We beheld his glory, the glory as of the only begotten of the Father.   JOHN 1:14

WE BEHELD
HIS GLORY

Sermons for the Advent Season
Christmas and New Year's Day

BY PASTORS OF
THE EVANGELICAL LUTHERAN CHURCH

Augsburg Publishing House · Minneapolis

Contents

"WE BEHELD HIS GLORY" ....Frontispiece
  Drawing by Lee Mero

FIRST SUNDAY IN ADVENT

WHEN JESUS COMES................ 3
  (Matthew 21:1-11)
  DR. GEORGE AUS, *Luther Theological Seminary,*
  St. Paul, Minnesota

THE KING OF LOVE................... 25
  (John 18:33-37)
  THE REV. F. I. SCHMIDT, *Bethel Lutheran*
  Church, Madison, Wisconsin

WHEN JESUS OPENED THE BOOK........ 39
  (Luke 4:16-22)
  THE REV. SIGURD T. SORENSON, *Salem Lutheran*
  Church, Glendale, California

SECOND SUNDAY IN ADVENT

WHENCE THIS LONGING?.............. 55
  (Luke 21:25-36)
  THE REV. ALVIN N. ROGNESS, *Trinity Lutheran*
  Church, Mason City, Iowa

THE SON OF MAN COMETH........... 65
  (Luke 12:35-40)
  DR. LAWRENCE M. STAVIG, *Augustana College,*
  Sioux Falls, South Dakota

THY KINGDOM COME................. 75
  (Luke 17:20-30)
  DR. HERMAN A. PREUS, *Luther Theological Sem-*
  inary, St. Paul, Minnesota

THIRD SUNDAY IN ADVENT

ART THOU HE THAT COMETH?......... 89
(Matthew 11:2-10)
THE REV. E. S. HJORTLAND, *Central Lutheran Church, Minneapolis, Minnesota*

GREAT MEN WHO MAKE US GREAT...... 99
(Matthew 11:11-15)
THE REV. JOSEPH L. KNUTSON, *Bethesda Lutheran Church, Ames, Iowa*

PRACTICAL REPENTANCE............... 111
(Luke 3:1-6)
DR. JOHN P. MILTON, *Luther Theological Seminary, St. Paul, Minnesota*

FOURTH SUNDAY IN ADVENT

THE VOICE OF ONE CRYING........... 125
(John 1:19-28)
DR. S. C. EASTVOLD, *Pacific Lutheran College, Parkland, Washington*

MAKE WAY FOR CHRIST!.............. 137
(John 3:22-36)
THE REV. JOSEPH SIMONSON, *Christ Lutheran Church, St. Paul, Minnesota*

THAT YE MIGHT BE SAVED............ 151
(John 5:31-39)
THE REV. SELMER A. BERGE, *The First Lutheran Church, Fargo, North Dakota*

CHRISTMAS DAY

GOD'S GREATEST GIFT................ 161
(Luke 2:1-14)
DR. J. A. AASGAARD, Minneapolis, Minnesota.
President, Evangelical Lutheran Church

SUNDAY AFTER CHRISTMAS

THEY KNEW HIM..................... 169
(Luke 2:33-40)
DR. MORRIS WEE, *Student Service Commission,
National Lutheran Council, Chicago, Illinois*

AND THE HOLY SPIRIT WAS UPON HIM... 181
(Luke 2:25-32)
THE REV. FREDRIK A. SCHIOTZ, *Trinity Lutheran
Church, Brooklyn, New York*

LESSONS FOR AFTER-CHRISTMAS.......... 191
(Luke 1:68-75)
THE REV. THEODORE HEIMARCK, *United Luther-
an Church, Red Wing, Minnesota*

NEW YEAR

SANCTIFIED MEMORIES AND GOOD HOPE.. 211
(Luke 2:21)
DR. T. F. GULLIXSON, *Luther Theological Sem-
inary, St. Paul, Minnesota*

OUR PRICELESS CHRIST IS FREE.......... 219
(John 1:16-18)
THE REV. OSCAR C. HANSON, *Young People's
Luther League, Minneapolis, Minnesota*

THIS YEAR ALSO..................... 233
(Luke 13:6-9)
THE REV. GERHARD E. FROST, *Luther College,
Decorah, Iowa*

And when they drew nigh unto Jerusalem, and came unto Bethphage, unto the mount of Olives, then Jesus sent two disciples, saying unto them, Go into the village that is over against you, and straightway ye shall find an ass tied, and a colt with her: loose them, and bring them unto me. And if any one say aught unto you, ye shall say, The Lord hath need of them; and straightway he will send them. Now this is come to pass, that it might be fulfilled which was spoken through the prophet, saying, Tell ye the daughter of Zion, Behold, thy King cometh unto thee, meek, and riding upon an ass, and upon a colt, the foal of an ass. And the disciples went, and did even as Jesus appointed them, and brought the ass, and the colt, and put on them their garments; and he sat thereon. And the most part of the multitude spread their garments in the way; and others cut branches from the trees, and spread them in the way. And the multitudes that went before him, and that followed, cried, saying, Hosanna to the son of David: Blessed is he that cometh in the name of the Lord; Hosanna in the highest. And when he was come into Jerusalem, all the city was stirred, saying, Who is this? And the multitudes said, This is the prophet, Jesus, from Nazareth of Galilee.

MATTHEW 21:1-11

Chapter One

When Jesus Comes

HAVE you ever noticed how curious the average city person is? It doesn't take much to gather a crowd in a city. Every street corner vendor, no matter what kind of gadget he's trying to sell, gets an audience. Each new construction job has its quota of "sidewalk engineers." The siren of a fire engine is sure to start a stream of people running in its direction.

If we would keep this fact in mind whenever we read today's text it would help make the historic situation come to life again.

Jerusalem wasn't a big city as modern cities go, but it was urban enough to have the restive character that marks city dwellers. The people of the capital city were used to having pilgrims streaming through its gates at the times of the great national festivals. They were accustomed to hearing the enthusiastic singing of the Psalms of Ascent by the zealots as they approached the temple city.

But when the pilgrim company numbered several hundreds and its members were tearing branches from the trees and spreading them before a man riding on a donkey, even taking off their outer garments and laying them on the ground so they could form a carpet for Him to ride on, and when the sounds that rent the air were not those of the Psalms of Ascent but the enthusiastic hailing of the rider as one who came "in the name of the Lord," then curiosity was aroused and all Jerusalem became astir.

Can't you see them as they come running—out of every alley and from every direction—calling to others as they come, with but a single question in their minds and on their lips, "Why all the excitement?" only to have the first question replaced by another as soon as they discover that the attention of the pilgrims is focussed on the man astride the donkey, "Who is this?"

Even though only one of the answers to their second question was spoken, in reality three answers were given.

The spoken answer was that given by the pilgrims. "Don't you folks know who this man is? Haven't you heard of the mighty things he has done? This is the prophet, Jesus, from Nazareth of Galilee!" There was a note of conviction in their ready response, a conviction born of, and nourished by, that which they had seen and heard. This was the man who had fed over five thousand people with a few loaves and a handful of fish. This was the man who had caused the blind beggar to see again. This was the man who had called

Lazarus out of the grave. No one could be a witness to such amazing manifestations of power without drawing the conclusion that here was a more than ordinary man. The words that Nicodemus used at the beginning of his interview with Jesus put as nicely as any words can the popular sentiment about Jesus: "We know that thou art a teacher come from God; for no one can do these signs that thou doest, except God be with him." The pilgrims' answer to the question, "Who is Jesus?" was clear and concise: "He is a prophet—a man sent by God!"

The second answer, one of those unspoken, was that given by the religious leaders. In the paragraph following our text we are told that when the procession reached the temple Jesus entered it and drove out the money changers and those who were using it as a place of merchandise. Through all of this the earlier enthusiasm of the pilgrims evidently continued unabated because we read that when the chief priests saw what Jesus was doing and heard the children crying, "Hosanna to the Son of David," they became very angry and called on Him to stop them. Implied in this action is their answer to the question, "Who is this?" Their conclusion about Jesus was that He was an impostor. No man of God would do what He had done. He had acted as though the observance of the ceremonial laws was a matter of indifference. He had paid more attention to the poor and the outcasts than He had to them, the vested authorities in church and state. And now, to top it all, He had publicly condemned, both in word and by deed, religious practices which had their origin in the very ordinances of Moses himself. The answer of the Pharisees to the question, "Who is Jesus?" was equally clear and concise: "He is an impostor, a man who must be done away with."

The third answer, the other of the unspoken ones, was given by Jesus Himself. For almost three years now He had been preaching and teaching and healing. One of the intents that ran through all this activity was the desire to make known His identity and mission. He could not come right out in the open and say so in so many words, because there were too many whose conceptions of the Messiah were wholly nationalistic and materialistic. To feed these fires would mean to ruin all chance of achieving His own ends. He therefore moved forward with great caution. By a word here and an action there He gradually disclosed to those to whom He wanted it revealed who He was. When Peter confessed Him as the Christ at Cæsarea Philippi, Jesus knew that one of the objectives of His ministry had been realized.

From that time on Jesus relaxed His former restraint and spoke and acted with far greater liberty about Himself. The situation in our text is an outstanding illustration. Centuries before the prophet Zechariah had told his people that the King they longed for, the King who would usher in the long-awaited era of peace and righteousness, would come to them not as a mighty warrior, a monarch crushing all resistance before him, but meek and lowly and riding upon a "colt the foal of an ass." In making a final appeal to Jerusalem, Jesus determined to make a literal fulfillment of this prophecy. They had asked Him to tell them plainly whether He was the Christ or not. He would now tell them with such clarity that only such as were unwilling could help understanding what He was trying to say. Jesus' answer to the question "Who is this?" was also clear and concise, "I am Messiah, the Christ of God."

While in one sense Jesus' answer was an answer to the question of His identity, in another sense it was more a disclosure of His mission than of His person. Just as the word "president" is a functional title, a title designating a certain work to be done, so also is the title Christ. The Christ was not primarily *to be someone* but *to do something*. His was a mission to perform.

What was His mission? What was it He was trying to accomplish? There have been many attempts to answer that question down through the centuries. Some have maintained that His mission was that of a teacher, the greatest spiritual teacher of all time, giving to mankind the most satisfying answers to its deepest questions. Others have championed the view that His work was that of a trail-blazer in the realm of human behavior. He stands as the paragon of human conduct for all time. He has set us the example. Our duty is but to follow "in His steps." Still others have claimed that His work was that of a reformer, a champion of inherent human rights. The forces of ignorance, prejudice, and selfish privilege had held sway for centuries. Under this load the human spirit was crushed and broken and on the verge of succumbing. As over against the situation as He found it, Jesus' work was to smash the fetters that held the spirit of man in bondage and to set it free. Our duty as His followers is to be eternally on guard against any re-enslavement of man's spirit.

What shall we say to all these claims? Our best answer is a question, a question directed not at these claims but to Jesus. He ascribed to Himself the title Christ. How did He conceive of His mission? What answer does He give to the question about the work of the Messiah? In the verse that forms the very heart of Luke's gospel, chapter 19, verse 10, Jesus, using His own synonym for Messiah, says, "The Son of Man came to seek and to save that which was lost."

As we watch Jesus at work in the pages of the New Testament and in the church today we discern three phases in His mission of seeking and saving. When Jesus comes He comes to make known to us our urgent need; He comes to reveal Himself as the Savior we need; and He comes to share with us His own character.

When is a man lost? The fifteenth chapter of Luke's gospel contains three of Jesus' best-known parables: the lost sheep, the lost coin, and the lost son. The sheep was lost because it was not where it belonged—with the flock and in the fold. The coin was lost because it was not where it was supposed to be—in its owner's possession. The prodigal was lost because he was away from his father's house. In these parables we have the mind of

Scripture on the word "lost." In Scripture a man is lost when he is not rightly related to God. A man out of fellowship with God is a lost man.

Does that mean that a man is lost only when he is where the prodigal was—down and out and in the gutter? Not at all! A man may be in the midst of plenty and yet be lost.

In the basement of an apartment house in one of our large cities lived a widow and her three children. By cleaning halls she kept her family under one roof and by scrubbing clothes she managed to keep them clothed and fed. One of her duties as caretaker was to collect the rents. Each month the landlord would roll up in his limousine to get the rents she had collected. On one of these visits he pointed to one of the children and said to the mother, "Why don't you let me take her home with me? I can give her everything her little heart desires." The mother's immediate response was, "No, thank you. My children are all I have in this life. I would sooner die than give up any one of them."

This happened for several months. The continued repetition of the offer worked on the mother's mind. Could it be that her first impulse was prompted by selfishness? Surely the landlord was right. He could give her little girl much more than she ever could. If she grew up in his home she never would lack anything. The more she considered the more she came to the conclusion that in the interest of her child the right thing for her to do would be to accept the landlord's invitation.

On his next visit the landlord repeated the invitation. To his great surprise he received the answer for which he had secretly hoped. It wasn't long before little Judith was being taken in the big limousine to a mansion overlooking the harbor. Once inside she was shown her bedroom. When her eyes had drunk enough of its beauty and comfort she was taken to a playroom, a room filled with all the things a child's heart would want. Her little eyes grew big with astonishment and her little heart fairly burst with joy at the thought that this was hers—all hers.

To begin with her attention was so taken up by all the things she saw and experienced that she had no time to miss anything. But had you been in the house about four-thirty that afternoon you would have heard the patter of little feet running from room to room and the plaintive voice of a little girl crying, "I want my Mommie. I want my Mommie." In the midst of plenty the little one was lost!

Grown-ups can be like that, too. Zaccheus, for instance, was like that. He was head of the internal revenue office in his city. As such he had a very handsome income and he lived in keeping with it. Despite the fact that he had been disowned by the church he was a man of considerable influence in the community. At first he was thrilled by the possession of things. Money, comfort, position—these constituted life for him! But after awhile those things began to pall on him. There were other values in life. Values which money couldn't buy. Values without which life was merely existence. Down deep in his heart

Zaccheus felt an aching void and his soul cried out to have it filled.

Maybe it's that way with you, too. I do not know who you are. After all, only the Holy Spirit really knows our hearts. You had religious training, grew up where you went to Sunday school, are confirmed perhaps. Then along came adolescence. You came into an enlarging world, a world filled with things, new people, sights, and thrills that held your attention and drew you along. For a time you didn't miss anything. The new-found experiences and the fascination of things occupied you to the exclusion of all else. But that's worn off now and there you sit. You are a respectable person in the community. You have a nice home and you are surrounded by comfort and by plenty of things and yet you are not satisfied. Your soul is not at rest. Somewhere along the line you parted company with God and now your heart cries out in much the same fashion as little Judith's, even though you may not fully understand its language. In your present condition you are not rightly related to God and you know it!

Now, the tragedy of being spiritually lost is the fact that, until God's Spirit causes us to see, we don't really appreciate our plight. We may have a deep-seated anxiety about ourselves but it is never allowed to become articulate as long as we are fascinated by power, possession, or pleasure. In order to show us our real condition Jesus comes in quest of us. When Jesus comes we see ourselves as we really are.

That's the way it was with Peter. He was no

doubt an average man, no worse and no better than his neighbor, a normal citizen of his community. But when he came face to face with Jesus he saw himself in a new light. We don't know all the details of what happened on that occasion when Jesus and Peter were out fishing together, but we do know that when Peter got to shore he fell at Jesus' feet and cried, "Depart from me, Lord, for I am a sinful man." He had met the Master face to face and in that meeting depths of his being came to view of which he had not been cognizant earlier. When Jesus comes He reveals to us our need of a Savior.

That's the way it was with the rich young ruler, too. By every one else's judgment he was an exemplary young man. He even believed it himself. He had never stolen. He revered his parents. He had not sought sensual pleasures. He had not sworn deceitfully. Yet, when he came face to face with Jesus he was weighed in the balance and found himself wanting. The fact that he was unwilling to accept the invitation of Jesus does not alter the fact that when Jesus met him he saw himself as he really was—a proud and self-centered young man. When Jesus comes we see ourselves as we really are.

Perhaps it's that way with you, too! Once you could sin with comparative ease, but now your sins bother you. Once you were not a bit concerned about God, but now the thought of meeting God terrifies you. Once you were quite sure of yourself and of your ability to get by, but now you realize that you won't make it as you are and you are in despair because in spite of your best efforts you get worse.

My friend, do you know what that is? That is Jesus seeking you, for when Jesus comes seeking He causes us to see ourselves as we really are, not rightly related to God—lost!

But, thanks be to God, when Jesus comes He has more in mind than to show us our lost condition —otherwise there would be no way out of the valley of our despair. When Jesus comes He does not only show us that we need a Savior but He also reveals Himself as the Savior that we need.

What is it that causes two people to be not rightly related to each other? How does it happen that two people come to be "on the outs"? That happens when one of the parties involved does something which is contrary to the rights or the will of the other. Such a situation arises when one of the persons wrongs the other.

A Christian student attending a university rented a room from a middle-aged couple. He had not been in the home for many days before he realized that all was not well between man and wife. As the weeks rolled by this situation became a burden which he took to the Lord in prayer each day asking for an opportunity to help.

One afternoon while he was in the midst of his studies the lady of the house knocked on the door of his room and asked whether she might see him. They had not conversed very long before the woman began to unburden her heart. Before retirement her husband had been a traveling man. Away from home much of the time, he had been unfaithful to her. In ways which she did not disclose she had learned of his broken vows. After much struggle she came to the place where she was really willing to forgive him. At an opportune time she made known to him that she knew what had happened and expressed her desire to forgive and to forget. To her great consternation her husband, instead of admitting his guilt and humbly asking for pardon, acted as though what he had done was entirely within his rights. From that day on there had been a wall between them. They lived together under the same roof, ostensibly man and wife, but they were no longer rightly related to each other.

What has to happen in such a situation before a reconciliation can be effected? Peace will be restored when, on the one hand, the party who has done the wrong is willing to make a full acknowledgment of guilt and to take whatever consequences there may be and, on the other hand, when the party wronged is willing to forgive the offender and to bear the cost of forgiveness.

That's the way it is between God and us, too. What the first impact of Jesus' coming does is to show us that we have offended God.

God made us for fellowship with Himself, but we turned our backs on God. Instead of seeking His will we have gone our own willful ways. Instead of trusting Him we have looked to ourselves and our own devices. Instead of living in the best interest of our fellow man we have sought to use Him for our own selfish ends. No wonder God is offended! Little wonder that we are not rightly related to Him!

This means that the situation is the way it is because of me. I am the guilty party. And as the guilty one, I deserve to be punished. There are inevitable consequences of my action.

It is the recognition of the correctness of this line of thinking that drives me deeper into the valley of despair. "I have sinned. God is going into judgment with me. There isn't anything I can do to remedy the situation or to avert what is coming because the condemnation is deserved."

It is *then* that the Gospel is good news. It is to such ears that the words, "God sent not his Son into the world to condemn the world but that the world might be saved through him," seem too good to be true.

In the midst of the 1929 depression a little old lady from Norway came to one of the sea coast missions conducted by our church. Fortunately the man in charge could speak Norwegian so he understood her story. It went somewhat as follows:

Some twenty-five years earlier a son had been born into their home. As the years went by, several other children joined the family circle. When the oldest was thirteen the father died. A year later the first-born was confirmed and not many months after set out for the sea. The first year he remembered his mother's parting admonition and wrote regularly, sending home what money he could. In the course of the second year there was a marked change. He wrote only once in a while and then very briefly. By the time the third year rolled around he had stopped writing altogether.

Though broken-hearted, his mother never gave up hope. In conversation with others she always excused him. In private she prayed for him night and day.

Since the last word she had had from him was from America she made it her business to ask all who came to those parts on a visit from America whether they had by chance seen her son. One man, not wanting to quench the dying embers of hope in her breast, suggested that he might be at X Mission.

Hope burst into flame anew. As she pondered the suggestion a plan of action formed itself in her breast. Her other children were now married and could take care of themselves. She would sell her little homestead and go to America in quest of her lost son.

Not long after she came to X Mission. Over the protests of those in charge she placed herself at the entrance of the mission. Of everyone who entered she asked, "Har du set gutten min?" (Have you seen my boy?) Days grew into weeks and weeks into months, and then one day mother and son met on the steps of the mission.

God is like that! That is what the gospel tells us and what the Holy Spirit working through that gospel assures us. Just as the shepherd risks his life on the mountain side to find his lost sheep, just as this little old lady sold all she had and came to strange shores in quest of her son, so God

comes to us in Christ seeking to effect a reconciliation.

That, my brother, is why Jesus comes to you
today. He comes to tell you that when He died
on Calvary He died for your sins; that He died
that you might be forgiven; that He died that
you might be saved from your present condition
and be restored to fellowship with God. He comes
to you now offering you the forgiveness of sins and
assuring you that the way is open for you to receive it.

Deacon Larsen was making his rounds in X hospital having devotions with the sick of the congregation. As he came to one bed the deaconess
on duty said that there wasn't much use reading
for this patient because she was delirious most of
the time. The deacon was a little hard of hearing
so he didn't quite catch what had been said and
proceeded to sit down by the bedside and read
from his New Testament. He read from the sixth
chapter of John. When he got to the thirty-
seventh verse, the sick woman was fully conscious
—"and him that cometh unto me I will in no wise
cast out."

At that point she must have slipped back into
unconsciousness again because when she came to
again all she remembered was those words from
the thirty-seventh verse—"and him that cometh
unto me I will in no wise cast out." It seemed as
though they had been burned into her soul.

She had not been a bad woman, no better nor
worse than the rest. But she had let the cares of
this life choke what had been planted in child-

hood. For the last year or so, however, she had gone to church out of concern for her son who was soon to go for confirmation. As a result of the hearing of the Word she had come under convicting power of the Holy Spirit. She admitted that all that He said about her was true, but she had difficulty believing that God wanted anything to do with someone like her.

Now, however, she could doubt no longer. The Word of the Lord told her that His death availed for her and that she could come as she was. And there on a little bed in the female ward of X hospital she committed herself to His saving grace in the words of a stanza she had heard in church.

> Just as I am without one plea,
> But that Thy blood was shed for me,
> And that Thou bidst me come to Thee,
> O Lamb of God, I come, I come.

Now, while it is true that Jesus' immediate purpose in coming to us is to re-establish personal fellowship between Himself and us, yet even this is a means to an end in His hand, for by having us live in communion with Him He purposes to share His character with us. Where Jesus comes He makes men like Him.

According to Scripture God created man that he might be like Him and be blessed forever. Accordingly, when He created man He created him for fellowship with Him and endowed him with all the resources necessary for the maintenance and growth of that relationship.

But tragedy stalked the garden. Instead of re-

maining in the fellowship of the heavenly Father
man revolted and went "on his own." As a result,
the life of fellowship was broken. The rich native
endowment was corrupted and the lofty destiny
which was his in design was forfeited.

Man's revolt, however, did not deter God. In
due season a second Adam appeared on the human scene—the Word become flesh: where the
first Adam fell the second stood. In Jesus of Nazareth, God's idea of man was realized. Here was a
man who in all things put God first. His own comfort, His own wishes, His own position—these
were all secondary. The number one priority in
His life was His Father's will. Similarly, here was
a man who in all things acted in the best interest
of His fellow man. Man-made tradition and prejudice, personal discomfort or disadvantage—none
of these were permitted to hinder Him from living a life of love toward those whom He was not
ashamed to call His brethren.

What Jesus accomplished by His perfect manhood, however, was not in His own interest but
in ours. Jesus Christ is the means by which God
proposes to share His character with us. This is
what Paul means when he calls Jesus the wisdom
of God. Christ Jesus is the means by which God
proposes to realize His redemptive purpose. And
this is what the writer of the Epistle to the He-
brews means when he writes: "For it became him,
for whom are all things and through whom are all
things, in bringing many sons to glory to make
the author of their salvation perfect through sufferings." God is going to bring many sons to glory

by bringing them into conformity with the image of His Son.

But how does God propose to carry this out? By bringing men into vital personal fellowship with Jesus Christ and by having them live in that relationship. As men live in fellowship with Jesus Christ they are being transformed into His likeness; they share in His character. This is what Paul means when he writes in II Corinthians 3:18, "But we all, with unveiled face, beholding as in a mirror the glory of the Lord, are transformed into the same image from glory to glory, even as from the Lord the Spirit."

Among the first whom Jesus called to be disciples were two brothers—James and John. They were sons of a fisherman who was rather well-off. Their mother was a woman who was ambitious on her sons' behalf. The few glimpses that we have of her in the New Testament indicate that she was on the lookout for the promotion of her sons' best interests. The boys evidently had things pretty much their own way. Those who knew them well had given them the nickname "Sons of Thunder" because of their quick tempers.

Into His fellowship Jesus called these two young men. They joined His ranks at once. There is no indication in the gospels, however, that there was any momentary change in their character. On the contrary, there are several indications that their fiery tempers continued to flare up. On one occasion when it became known that there were others than the disciples of Jesus who were performing mighty deeds in His name they asked,

"Shall we call down fire from heaven to devour them?"

While it is true that admission into the group of disciples made no sudden change in their characters, there is plenty of evidence in the New Testament that as they continued to live in the fellowship of Jesus their lives were transformed. What is John's name later on? Son of Thunder? No! Apostle of Love! The same man who years before was so hot-tempered that he earned for himself the nickname Son of Thunder is now so Spirit-tempered that he bears the title Apostle of Love. He who once wanted to call down fire from heaven on others now admonishes, "My little children, love one another."

This transforming power of Christ is not just a chapter concluded in the past. Wherever men live in fellowship with Him there He is at work sharing His character with them. Have we not all seen it? Anyone who has been connected with a Christian congregation long enough to become acquainted with its members has met them—older folks who have lived with the Lord for many years and become mature Christian personalities. No, they aren't perfect. They still have faults. They continue to find that they need to pray each day for the forgiveness of sins. But the fact that they have lived together with Jesus in word and sacrament, in prayer and obedience, has left its unmistakable mark upon them. Not all started with the same temperaments; nor did all have the same privileges and opportunities in life; nor did all have identical experiences. But they were all met by the same Christ whose purpose for all was the same, namely, that through living together with Him they might share His character. To the extent that they have lived together with Him they have come to be "little Christs," becoming both salt and light in the church and in the community.

What has happened in the lives of individuals can also be seen in the life of a nation. Once the people of France prayed in effect, "Almighty God, protect us from the scourge of the Vikings." Would the people of France think of offering such a prayer today? Of course not! Why not? Because the Vikings have been transformed into one of the most peace-loving and good-neighborly peoples of the earth. How has this transformation come about? By the power of the gospel of Jesus Christ! This does not mean that all of the descendants of the Vikings are Christians, nor that those who are have already been made perfect, but it does mean that enough of them have come into His saving fellowship to make such an impact on the life of Norway as to revolutionize it.

In a day when suspicion and fear are once more the dominant notes in the international situation, the Rider, who has not yet mounted His white charger, still rides on errands of mercy—O earth, earth, earth—behold and hear the Word of the Lord!

In the quiet of this hour of worship Jesus has been here on errands of mercy. He has come to make known to us our need of salvation. He has come to reveal Himself as the Savior we need and

to invite us to receive Him into our lives. He has
come to make us partakers of His holiness.

> Jesus Christ is passing by,
> Sinner, lift to Him thine eye;
> As the precious moments flee,
> Cry, "Be merciful to me."
>
> Lo, He stands and calls to thee,
> "What wilt thou then have of me?"
> Rise, and tell Him all thy need;
> Rise, He calleth thee indeed.
>
> Lord, I would Thy mercy see;
> Lord, reveal Thy love to me;
> Let it penetrate my soul,
> All my heart and life control.
>
> O how sweet the touch of power
> Comes—and is salvation's hour:
> Jesus gives from guilt release,
> "Faith hath saved thee, go in peace."
>
> AMEN

Pilate therefore entered again into the prætorium, and called Jesus, and said unto him, Art thou the King of the Jews? Jesus answered, Sayest thou this of thyself, or did others tell it thee concerning me? Pilate answered, Am I a Jew? Thine own nation and the chief priests delivered thee unto me: what hast thou done? Jesus answered, My kingdom is not of this world: if my kingdom were of this world, then would my servants fight, that I should not be delivered to the Jews: but now is my kingdom not from hence. Pilate therefore said unto him, Art thou a king then? Jesus answered, Thou sayest that I am a king. To this end have I been born, and to this end am I come into the world, that I should bear witness unto the truth. Every one that is of the truth heareth my voice.

LUKE 18:33-37

Chapter Two

The King of Love

THE Advent season is that season of the church year in which the hearts of Christian people are to be prepared for the coming Christmas festivities. It is a season which looks forward to the Babe of Bethlehem's manger crib. It directs the attention of men to the Wonder Child of the ages.

When a little child is born, the question is often asked: "What will this child become?" As men view with reverent adoration the humble little Child cradled in a manger, they may wonder what this Child of Mary's is to become.

This passage of scripture answers that question. The little child Jesus is to become a king, for to this end was He born and for this cause He came into the world. This heaven-sent King came into the world to bear witness to the truth. He was to become a King of grace whom heaven sent into the world to seek and to save that which was lost. He was to be a King of Love, who would seek to win the allegiance of the hearts of men and would seek to rule their lives.

Shortly after Pilate had questioned Jesus as to His kingship, he turned Jesus over to the rough soldiers, who mocked His claim to being a King. They would show men what they thought of Jesus the King. They, like many today, would have no king but Caesar. Yet in this pitiable picture of human perversity we have a prophetic picture of the King of Love. With cruel hands the soldiers stripped Jesus and put on Him a scarlet robe, prophetic of that robe of righteousness which He would provide for all His followers. Upon His head they platted a crown of thorns, prophetic of the fact that through bearing our griefs and carrying our sorrows, He would provide a crown of life for those who believed on Him. They put a reed in His hand, prophetic of Jesus' rule. They then led Jesus to Calvary's hill and gave Him the only throne the King of Love had in this world, a cross. Yet from that cross Jesus has won the allegiance of more souls than any earthly king who has sat upon a jewel bedecked throne.

No earthly king has ever had the matchless power of the King of Love. Earthly rulers may display their pomp and glory to dazzle the eyes of men, but none can compare with the wondrous glory of the King of Love

Jesus Is a King of Humble Character

Great men have strutted across the stage of history with a pompous display of military power and might, but no one in all history can compare with the character of Jesus. All through His life, from His birth to His resurrection, there is a loftiness of moral character that no man can ever dream of attaining. And yet our little children singing their Christian hymns will tell us of the beauty and heavenly glory of the character of Jesus. Listen to a group of Sunday school children singing "Beautiful Savior," and they will tell you that the beauty of their Savior far surpasses the glory, majesty and beauty of all creation.

Viewing the character of Jesus we are lost in wonder and reverent awe as we behold His goodness, wisdom, kindness and matchless love. But the sublime marvel of Jesus' character is His humility. Truly, He was meek and lowly in heart. Men saw only a common man, a humble servant of God. His divine majesty and glory were veiled from the eyes of men. Only as they saw His eternal glory break through, as it did on the Mount of Transfiguration, did they realize the dazzling majesty that was tabernacled in that house of human clay.

The apostle Paul, referring to this side of Jesus' character, said: "Ye know the grace of the Lord Jesus Christ, that, though he was rich, yet for your sake he became poor, that ye through his poverty might be rich." Again in Philippians Paul says: "Who being in the form of God, thought it not robbery to be equal with God; but made himself of no reputation and took upon himself the form of a servant and was made in the likeness of men; and being found in fashion as a man he humbled himself and became obedient unto death, even the death of the cross." The perfect man, the God-man, yet the humble man.

Jesus, the King of Love, met scorn and insult in the spirit of humility. Men mocked His place of birth, they ridiculed Him as only the son of Joseph, the carpenter. When men reviled Him, He reviled not again. They crucified Him on a cross, but as the cruel nails were pounded into His quivering flesh, above the sound of the hammer were heard the words of a prayer for His enemies. His eyes blazed with indignation at the injustice and cruelty that were shown to others. He spoke words of condemnation to those whose hearts were filled with hypocrisy and greed. But when He Himself was mocked, scourged, spat upon and crowned with thorns, He opened not His mouth, as a lamb led to the slaughter He was dumb.

Christian people who claim to be the subjects of this humble King of Love should have the same regal spirit which marks their King.

> Just stand aside and watch yourself go by,
> Think of yourself as "He" instead of "I."
> Pick flaws, find fault, forget the man is you.
> And try to make the estimate ring true.
>
> The faults of others then will dwarf and shrink.
> Love's chain grows stronger by one mighty link
> When you with "He" as substitute for "I"
> Have stood aside and watched yourself go by.

As Christians, we are the sons and daughters of the King. We should be like Him and bear the family likeness, as Paul says in Phil. 2:5: "Let this mind be in you which was also in Christ Jesus." The King's spirit and nature should be our spirit and nature. Therefore, all conceit and pride must be rooted out of our hearts by the help of God. We should not carry our heads high with a haughty air of superiority. We should not be arrogant, exacting and unforgiving. Rather, Christ's spirit of gentleness, forgiveness and kindness should mark our walk as the children of the King.

Jesus Is a King of Love

The conquest of Christ over nations and peoples has been the marvel of history. The advancement of His kingdom throughout the world to the day when the kingdoms of this world shall become His kingdom is the amazement of men. Christianity marched out of the little country of Palestine to conquer the military power of Rome, the culture of Greece, the barbarianism of Europe and the paganism of the Orient. And it is alone by the power of love that Christ's kingdom makes its advance over all the world.

Jesus never organized armies or waged war to master men by staining the earth with blood and filling the lives of men with tears and sorrow. The only blow struck with a weapon in His behalf was struck by Peter in the garden of Gethsemane, and Jesus sternly rebuked such a procedure. The power of Jesus is not the power of guns and tanks, armies and navies, bombs and poison gas, but only the power of a divine love that yearns to save men and bring to men the abundant and eternal life. He refused to make the strength of His kingdom depend upon material wealth, human influence or social standing. The learned and cultured Nicodemus was plainly told that he must be born again if he would enter the kingdom of God. The gates of Christ's kingdom open alone to those of a repentant spirit and a contrite heart. The only means Jesus used to further His kingdom was a lowly life, a divine message of God's grace and a cross of shame.

What a terrible mistake the Christian Church makes when it thinks that if it could only get the "big" men, the men of influence, wealth and power, then the kingdom of Christ would soon cover the earth. Christ refuses every power save that of consecrated Christian love, but He can use all things of this world to further His cause when they are dedicated to Him in a spirit of sacrificial love. Truly, the Lord had need of the beast of burden upon which to ride into Jerusalem for His coronation. Truly, the Lord had need of the room of a friend in which to gather with His disciples to eat the last Passover feast together. Truly, the Lord had need of the home of Martha and Mary and Lazarus in which to rest from His strenuous labors. And the Lord hath need today of men and women of talent, means and ability with which to further His cause. But our Lord is not dependent upon these forces alone. He can do without them if He must. But He can also gloriously use them when they are consecrated to Him in the spirit of true Christian love.

When He who was King and Lord of all creation came to this world, the world had no room for Him, but He was willing to enter into this world by being born in a lowly stable. When friends forgot to provide a place for Him, He betook Himself to the Mount of Olives to spend the night there in prayer and communion with His Father. When all men forsook Him and fled, He trod the winepress alone. When men refused to give Him His rightful throne, the throne of David, He was willing to reign from a cross.

We look out upon a world today that is in travail giving birth to a new age. Which force shall predominate in this new age, the force of brute power or of Christian love, depends upon whether the Christian people of the world are going to be willing to consecrate all things into the hands of their Lord, that He might use both them and the things they have to bring in His kingdom of love to rule over the hearts and minds of men. May the Christians of the world follow Christ humbly and faithfully and permit His spirit to guide and empower them that Christ's kingdom might triumph gloriously over all the forces of evil so dominant in the world today.

Jesus Is a King of Grace

The Lord does not deal with men according to their sins or their just deserts, but in grace. Grace is showing kindness and forgiveness to the undeserving.

In grace Jesus dealt with the woman of Samaria whose soul had become stricken with spiritual drought. Jesus opened for her the fountains of living water, whereby the thirst of her soul was eternally satisfied. In grace Jesus brought bread to the hungry multitudes even as He today brings the bread of life to those who hunger and thirst after righteousness. In grace Jesus dealt with the widow of Nain as her heart was broken and shadowed with sorrow over the loss of her only son even as He brings the word of life to the dying children of men and the word of hope to those who stand beside the graves of their departed loved ones. In grace Jesus dealt with the woman taken in adultery, becoming her defender against her bigoted and self-righteous accusers. To her He spoke the word of forgiveness: "Go and sin no more." Every sinner who comes to Him in repentance and faith Jesus deals with in grace and gives pardon for sin. In grace Jesus dealt with the thief on the cross and opened for him the doors of the kingdom of eternal life. Grace flowed from the life of Jesus to men in healing the sick, giving sight to the blind, raising the fallen, forgiving the sinner, and bringing life to the dead.

A little ragged boy in one of our larger cities was in an automobile accident and was brought to a hospital to be treated. The next day a nurse came and offered the youngster a large glass of milk. The boy came from a poor family with many children, among whom everything had to be shared. Accepting the glass of milk from the nurse, he said to her: "Nurse, how deep can I drink?" The poor little fellow thought there were others with whom he should share his milk. The nurse looked at him and said: "Why bless you, my boy, you may drink as deep as you want." And so it is with the grace of God in Christ Jesus. There's a wideness in God's mercy like the wideness of the sea. We may drink deeply of His grace to satisfy our every need and want. God's grace is sufficient for us and for all mankind.

How wonderful is the grace of Jesus, the King of Love. Eternity will be too short a time to tell the story of the wonders of His grace. And those who stand before the throne of God will sing the glory song of those who were saved by grace and grace alone.

Jesus always deals in grace with His sinning and erring disciples. When He was gathered with His disciples in that holy sacramental hour in the upper room, the hearts of the disciples were filled with pride, self-importance and dissension. Then Jesus took a towel and a basin of water and began to wash the disciples' feet. By that act He taught them the true way to greatness, that he who would be the greatest among men must be the servant of all. Here Jesus the King, girded with a towel, not a sword, was performing the menial task of a servant, pointing all men to the true path of greatness, that of Christian service.

In grace Jesus dealt with erring and sinning Peter, who sinned so grievously in denying his Lord. He did not rebuke him with scathing words, but with a look of wounded love He turned and looked at Peter. That look melted poor Peter's heart and he went out and wept bitter tears of repentance. Thus Christ deals with men today in mercy, grace and forgiveness for all repentant souls. Thus Christ has dealt with you and me through the years. All His gracious dealings with us have been His way of winning our heart's love, wooing us from the paths of sin and unrighteousness, that we might be saved unto His eternal kingdom.

How graciously Jesus deals with all sinful men, bringing hope to the discouraged, comfort to the sorrowing, cheer to the despondent and assurance to the fearful. A man came to the home of a doctor and was met at the door by the doctor's little girl. "Is your father at home?" asked the man. "No, he's away," answered the little girl. "Where can I find him?" asked the man. The little girl replied: "You've got to look for him some place where people are sick, hurt or dying. He's helping somewhere." And in this world of sin and suffering and death Jesus went about doing good. He was always helping where people were sick, hurt or dying. He walks today throughout the world wherever men and women motivated by the spirit of Christ administer to the needs of their fellowmen. Jesus goes about doing good today whenever men and women in Christ's name administer to the sick and the dying, visit those who are in prison, give water to the thirsty, food to the hungry, or clothes to the naked. Thus Christ in our day can dispense His help to the needy children of men. Christian people are to be His mouth to speak the word of life to men. They are to be His feet to run His errands of mercy and love. They are to be His hands to serve their fellowmen.

God is certainly calling His church today to action, to awake from its lethargy, to go out into the world and advance the borders of His kingdom. Christ is calling the subjects of His kingdom to a sacrificial service in His name. As the nations mustered their manpower in the days of war, so Christ is calling all Christians as a mighty army to go forth and bring His peace to the hearts of all men.

We as Christians cannot simply be spectators to the great world drama being enacted before our eyes. We cannot be just onlookers as humanity walks along the road of life, carrying its heavy burdens of sin, suffering and death. We cannot just live in our house by the side of the road and watch the race of men go by.

We must follow our Lord and King and get out and walk with men in the roadway of life, and share with them life's struggles and sorrows. Oh, how the King of Love needs men and women who will follow in His train and seek in His name to alleviate the sins and sufferings of this old world, so that all men may know the love of God in Christ Jesus and the healing which is found in Christ for all the sins and woes of life. The subjects of the King of Love must be on a mighty crusade today to bring the peace and joy and hope of His kingdom to the hearts and lives of men.

Truly, the world sorely needs Jesus, the King of Love. Only Christ can meet the crisis of this age. The power of the atomic bomb can well destroy the world. The power of Christ can alone save the world. Our world is a reeling, staggering world. This is no time for an anemic religion, a washed out faith. This is the day for heroic, Christian souls to go forth in the name and power of their risen, victorious Lord and bring salvation to a dying world. The church needs men and women who have such a faith in Christ that they believe that Christ can save this world, that He is equal to every emergency. The world is filled with distrust, unrest, immorality, sin of every kind, suffering untold, hate, greed, ambition and burdens of every sort. But Christ can meet the present world crisis. Christ can save sinning, dying men. Christians, awake! Christians, arise! Christians, follow your King!

AMEN

And he came to Nazareth, where he had been brought up: and he entered, as his custom was, into the synagogue on the sabbath day, and stood up to read. And there was delivered unto him the book of the prophet Isaiah. And he opened the book, and found the place where it was written, The Spirit of the Lord is upon me, because he anointed me to preach good tidings to the poor: he hath sent me to proclaim release to the captives, and recovering of sight to the blind, to set at liberty them that are bruised, to proclaim the acceptable year of the Lord. And he closed the book, and gave it back to the attendant, and sat down: and the eyes of all in the synagogue were fastened on him. And he began to say unto them, Today hath this scripture been fulfilled in your ears. And all bare him witness, and wondered at the words of grace which proceeded out of his mouth.

LUKE 4:16-22

Chapter Three

When Jesus Opened the Book

THE Savior was standing in the pulpit that Sabbath morning in the synagogue of His boyhood town of Nazareth when He opened the Book.

All eyes were fixed on Him. They knew Him as Joseph's son. But they also knew that since He left home, His name had increasingly gathered fame. He had been down to the great city of Jerusalem. He had challenged the proud Pharisees, and driven the money-changers out of the temple. The learned Nicodemus had interviewed Him. And returning travelers brought great tales of His mighty miracles. Now He stood before them. Would they arise and greet Him with a mighty Hosanna? And would they with one voice welcome Him as the Messiah promised by the prophets?

Earlier that day they had watched Him as He walked down the streets of the old town. He may have paused now and then to look at some familiar landmark. But it was not for long. As usual on the Lord's Day, He went "as his custom was," to church. And there the people followed Him.

Is it not rather strange that there are those who claim to be followers of Christ who get out of step with Him on the Lord's Day? At least, they are not to be seen in His company when He crosses the threshold to enter the church. Ignoring the commandment to keep the day holy, they hurry off to some outing, or just loaf round the house with the Sunday paper. When Jesus says, "Follow me," and we say, "Yes, Lord," there can be no alternative but to follow God's Son on the Lord's Day to God's House. Over the doorway of the Christian Church the promise is still written: "Here I will meet with thee, and I will commune with thee." Those who call Christ Lord will be ready to confess with the Psalmist, "I was glad when they said unto me, Let us go into the House of the Lord."

As Jesus stood in the pulpit, all eyes fastened on Him, He took the Book. From it came the message of the day. It was not the book of man's wisdom. It was the divine Word of God. A great artist has painted the picture of an old woman reading the Bible. Her face is illuminated as though light radiated from the pages. The picture is called, "The Light." There *is* light on the pages of God's Book. It is the radiance of the Holy Spirit. As we read the Word of truth reverently, and with a little prayer for guidance, we are able to say, "In thy light we shall see light."

Having taken the Book, He opened it. However precious the binding, a closed Bible is a silent book. A traveler coming into far-off Tibet found the natives bowed down before an altar upon which rested an old book. It was the Bible. A generation before, a Christian missionary had gone that way and left the volume. The natives believed it to be a holy thing, and worshipped it. But it had no voice or message for their souls.

There are folks in our day who reverence the Bible, but it does not speak to them. Even though it may have a place of honor on the parlor table and receive an occasional dusting, the owners are not blessed by it, because they do not use it. In his old age, writing the concluding chapters to the New Testament, John, the beloved disciple, gives this promise, "Blessed is he that readeth, and they that hear the words of this prophecy, and keep those things that are written therein."

And having opened the Book, He found the place. He knew how to use the Scriptures. A man once came to the evangelist Torrey and complained that he could not believe the Bible because it contained contradictions. Handing the man a copy of the Bible, Pastor Torrey said, "Show me the place." Taking the book, the man fumbled aimlessly from page to page. He could not find the place. He did not know the Book or its message.

There may be parts of the Bible that we cannot easily understand, just as with so many other things in life. But this we know, that he who will read the book prayerfully, seeking the truth, will not fail to find the place marked by the Cross of Christ, that shows clearly the way of salvation. For the promise is, "Seek and ye shall find." There is a place in the Book for you.

Having found the place, Jesus read the words of the Prophet Isaiah foretelling the coming of the Messiah and His glad tidings of salvation. These are the words,

The Spirit of the Lord is upon me,
Because he anointed me to preach good tidings to the
    poor;
He hath sent me to proclaim release to the captives,
And recovery of sight to the blind,
To set at liberty them that are bruised,
To proclaim the acceptable year of the Lord.

Then, looking at His listeners, He said, "Today this Scripture is fulfilled in your hearing."

Jesus was telling these folks in Nazareth that He whom they knew as Joseph's son, and who now stood before them, was none other than the Messiah promised them by God's Word. Instead of wearing any outward emblem of authority, He was anointed with the greater power of the Holy Spirit. Looking at Him, they were seeing the long-expected Christ of God, the Redeemer of the world!

They could not see, as we can see, that the Cross on Calvary was His throne of grace; that the empty Easter grave was His insignia of victory over sin and death; and that His triumphant ascension into the skies crowned Him forever with all power as He took His place at the right hand of the eternal Father. Let it be said again, Jesus Christ is the Messiah, the world's only Redeemer. "For there is none other name under heaven, given among men, whereby we must be saved."

Years ago, a fine elderly gentleman used to come to my services on festival days. He said he was a Unitarian. One day I asked him, "Is it true that Unitarians believe that Jesus was just a man and not the divine Son of God?"

He answered, "Yes."

"And do you believe the New Testament?"

"Oh, yes," he replied.

"But when you read the story of Jesus in the New Testament, do you not get the impression that He is the best man that ever lived?" I asked.

For a moment he did not answer. Then he said, "There have been other good men; Socrates, for instance, and Marcus Aurelius."

"Quite true," I replied. "Without doubt Socrates was a great man. But the honest historian admits that his domestic life was not without blemish. I suppose that rules him out. Marcus Aurelius is called a noble Roman philosopher. But as an emperor he has the blood of hundreds of Christian martyrs on his hands. He, too, I believe, must be ruled out. I wonder, after all, if there ever has been anyone as good as Jesus?"

My friend answered, "No one, I guess."

"Then," said I, "if Jesus Christ according to your belief is the best man that ever lived, and He tells us again and again in the New Testament that He is the divine Son of God, why do you make the best man that ever lived a liar?"

He answered, "I do not know."

The great Gladstone, taking time out from a strenuous political campaign, sat down to write a man who had asked him if he believed in the divinity of Christ, "All that I write, and all that I hope, and all that I think is based on the divinity of Jesus Christ, the one certain hope of our poor wayward race."

He who declared, "I and the Father are one," also took time out to tell the learned Nicodemus, "For God so loved the world that he gave his only begotten Son, that whosoever believeth in him should not perish, but have eternal life." Happy are those who, like Andrew, can say, "We have found the Messiah."

The wonderful message of good tidings that Jesus announced that day came from God. Through the words of the prophet, He tried to make plain to the people why He had come.

He had come to preach good tidings to the poor. Who cares for the poor? The Scribes and the Pharisees did not. The proud philosophers of Greece and Rome did not. Who cares to go out and see a procession of men and women in rags? Jesus does! Behind the pinched cheek and the patched coat, Jesus sees a royal guest invited to sit at the wedding supper of the King's Son in heaven. The Gospel of God's grace is good for all the children of men for both time and eternity. Wherever the Kingdom of God has had progress, the poor have been lifted up, the serf and the slave have been set free, and the working man has found a new living wage.

But Christ speaks first of all to "the poor in spirit." To the lowly of heart He brings new life and hope. Whenever a son or daughter has wandered far away into the land of sin, finding disgrace instead of glory, a broken heart instead of the abundant life, and at the end the fear of death and judgment, Christ the Redeemer comes to proclaim the good tidings that the unwearied Father stands waiting at the gate, ready to reclaim and restore the lost soul to a new life by grace alone.

> Just as I am, Thou wilt receive,
> Wilt welcome, pardon, cleanse, relieve,
> Because Thy promise I believe,
> O Lamb of God, I come, I come!

He came to set at liberty the captive. There are many prisoners behind the bars. Shall we unlock the iron gate and set them free? The murderer, the prostitute, the pickpocket, the depraved and the vicious? Shall we let them out like an evil stream to pollute our streets? Not many of us would want to have our home near such an exit.

But if someone could enter the gloomy cell and declare, "By the power and the grace of God, I will set you free from your desire for violence and from your depraved appetites. I will weed out the growing seeds of jealousy and hatred within you, and I will put in their place the spirit of forgiveness and lovingkindness. I will cleanse the unchastity from your heart and plant instead the white lily of purity. I will bend your will away from that which is evil and incline it toward that which is good," our prisoners would then be free even before the jailer unlocked the gates. "If the Son shall make you free, ye shall be free indeed."

Some years ago, a man came to one of our pastors and asked if he would help him overcome the evil habit of strong drink. Said the pastor, "If you are in earnest and really mean business, and if you are willing to get down here on your knees and ask God to help you win the victory, and if you will honestly resolve to stay away from every place of temptation, you will be a free man."

From that day, rejoicing in Christ who helped him to overcome the habit, he walked, a free man.

"Thanks be to God, who giveth us the victory through our Lord, Jesus Christ."

Wherever Christ has come to set free the spirit of man, other freedoms have followed, both social and political. The Pilgrim Fathers with their Mayflower Compact, signed "in the presence of God and one another," translated their Christian liberty into the democracy of "the land of the free." As their own historian Bradford says, "One small candle may light a thousand, so the light here kindled hath shone to many, yea, in some sort to our whole nation." The Savior came that we might have life and that we might have it more abundantly.

He came to give sight to the blind. To be in darkness, to have the curtains of sight pulled down, shutting out the scenes of this great world, is sad. Christ opened the windows of sight to many who were blind. Yet His greatest mission was to open the eyes of those who lacked spiritual vision.

He is blind who sees only self and cannot see his brother in need; who can see the speck in another's eye but cannot see the beam in his own eye; who can see the earth and the stars but cannot see the Creator of the heavens and the earth. He is blind who can see the grave and the darkness but cannot see the grace of God and the glory of the gates of life beyond. He is blind who can see his sin but not Christ the Savior of sinners.

Said a man who had lost the sight of his eyes, but through this misfortune had found the Savior, "When I had the use of my eyes I could not see God. But when my eyes failed, by the grace of God I received spiritual vision. And now I rejoice in Christ my Savior. My loss has proved to be my gain." For such a man the words of the Psalmist must have a deep meaning, "The Lord is my light and my salvation."

He came to set at liberty them that are bruised. Christ is the great Restorer. Some years ago there was a great railroad wreck near one of our large cities. One Pullman car was smashed and all occupants killed. A great public funeral was held for all the victims. Relatives came to bid a last farewell. Mother, father, son, daughter, loved one, blinded by tears, bent over each casket in turn. Each casket, save one. It was that of an unknown stranger. No one paused there. Finally, toward the close of the service, a little old woman walked up to the casket of the stranger and said, "I will kiss you for your mother's sake."

You may be broken and forgotten, a stranger in this strange world; but there is One who will know you and who cares for you, no matter who you are or how badly sin may have bruised you. His name is the Friend of Sinners. His grace is all-sufficient to cleanse and heal. He is also called The Consoler. Do not run away from Him. Go to Him with all your grief. He gives comfort and light in the dark day of your deepest sorrow. Earth has no wound that He cannot heal.

> For he was wounded for our transgressions;
> He was bruised for our iniquities.
> The chastisement of our peace was upon him;
> And with his stripes we are healed.

He came to proclaim the acceptable year of the Lord. Every half-century the children of Israel celebrated the Year of Jubilee. The trumpet sounded; all debts were cancelled and all slaves set free. Christ came, sounding the silver trumpet of the Gospel. He proclaimed the promised season of God's divine mercy for repentant sinners. Now, through grace alone, man's sin can be cancelled and the soul set free to walk in newness of life. It was the world's greatest emancipation proclamation!

Is it possible that anyone can hear this great message and not accept it gladly and humbly and thankfully?

As Christ gave His glad tidings to the people in the synagogue of Nazareth that day, did they arise and salute Him and crown Him Lord of all?

At first they sat spellbound, unable to resist the charm of His divine personality, or the gracious message of His speech. And we believe some who heard Him accepted Him gladly. We think Mary, the faithful mother, probably was there, and some of the disciples. We know they loved Him with an undying love and went forth to serve Him hand and heart.

As for the rest, hot anger rose up within them. With false pride they reasoned that they could not accept this Joseph's son as the anointed Messiah. Where were His mighty miracles? His royal credentials? Hurrying out of the synagogue, they became a mad mob desperately trying to push Him headlong to destruction down over the cliff. "But," as St. Luke tells us, "he, passing through the midst of them, went his way."

And, as He went, an invisible glory passed from the synagogue of Nazareth.

There have always been those who have rejected Christ, some by idle indifference or frank skepticism, others by violence. Not infrequently proud men sitting in the seats of the scornful have gloried in trying to destroy both Him and His Church. But, as former ambassador to Russia, William C. Bullitt, so aptly remarks in his recent volume, *The Great Globe Itself,* "The Word of God is strong. Religion has a way of outlasting dictators and persecutions." In due time, the glory of those who seek to destroy the Anointed One of God will vanish as the chaff which the wind driveth away. God is not mocked.

Thank God there are those who have accepted Him. A noble company singing the songs of salvation have followed the banner of the Cross and carried this old world upward in righteousness toward God. There have been women like the gentle Mary who have said, "My spirit rejoiceth in God my Savior." There have been strong men of rock like Peter who have left all to follow Him saying, "Thou only hath the words of eternal life."

The way has not always been easy. But He who declared, "Blessed are ye when men shall persecute you for my sake," has ever been spiritually present to sustain and strengthen those who put their trust in Him.

We can see it in the courage of the valiant Polycarp who, rather than deny his great Lord, faced the flaming stake unafraid while praising God for having deemed him worthy "to be numbered among the martyrs and to drink the cup of Christ's sufferings unto the eternal resurrection of the soul and the body."

What about our own day? Does the Man of Nazareth still speak to us with authority? And do many respond to His call? The answer is that no one speaks with more authority, and many do respond to His call.

I take out an old photograph of a little church. Strange feelings touch my heart as I gaze on the faded picture. There is the quaint pulpit, and the font, and the altar, and the colored window. You say, "What have you there?" I reply, "This is the picture of the world's most beautiful church." You answer, "How can you say that? Look at the plain furniture, the worn carpet and the simple altar. How can you call this the world's most beautiful church?" I say, "To me it is. Because here I found my Savior. Here He came to me in holy Baptism. In the Holy Communion, as I knelt down, He gave me pardon for my sins and new strength for my soul. And from this old pulpit I heard Christ speak to me through the living Word of God. Here I beheld His glory—full of grace and truth. And I have loved Him and followed Him ever since."

Christ proclaims the same message today as He did in the days of His flesh. He may commune with us on the mountain or on the sea or behind some closed door. But in a special way He speaks to us today as He did in Nazareth long ago, in the House of God where are the means of grace.

Thank God there are those who gladly hear Him and follow Him. Young folks carrying school books, men in uniform, women in the home, folks in the field and in the market place call Him Lord and Master. Even now there are eager volunteers for the mission fields standing ready to go to the ends of the earth declaring,

> I'll go where you want me to go, dear Lord,
> O'er mountain or plain or sea.
> I'll do what you want me to do, dear Lord;
> I'll be what you want me to be.

On this First Sunday in Advent, Christ comes once more with the silver trumpet of the Gospel, and opens for us again the Book of God's Tidings. It is not the book of the wrath of God's judgment against sinful man. It is the Book of Life "whose leaves are for the healing of the nations," offering forgiveness of sins and salvation to every heart that hungers and thirsts after righteousness.

Gladly we accept His message, dedicating our lives anew to Him who gave His life for us.

And this we do as we reverently bow before Him with a little prayer for cleansing and guidance, a humble prayer that has helped many a burdened soul in the way of salvation.

> Search me, O God, and know my heart;
> Try me and know my thoughts;
> And see if there be any wicked way in me;
> And lead me in the way everlasting.

Then, surrendered to His love, with faith and without fear, we go forth carrying our light into a darkened world. And as we go we shall also carry with us, like the rays of the morning light, the glory of His benediction with the promise, *"Blessed are they that hear the word of God and keep it."*

> I heard the voice of Jesus say,
>   I am this dark world's Light;
> Look unto Me, thy morn shall rise,
>   And all thy day be bright.
> I looked to Jesus, and I found
>   In Him my star, my sun;
> And in that Light of Life I'll walk
>   Till travelling days are done.

AMEN

And there shall be signs in sun and moon and stars; and upon the earth distress of nations, in perplexity for the roaring of the sea and the billows; men fainting for fear, and for expectation of the things which are coming on the world: for the powers of the heavens shall be shaken. And then shall they see the Son of man coming in a cloud with power and great glory. But when these things begin to come to pass, look up, and lift up your heads; because your redemption draweth nigh. And he spake to them a parable: Behold the fig tree, and all the trees: when they now shoot forth, ye see it and know of your own selves that the summer is now nigh. Even so ye also, when ye see these things coming to pass, know ye that the kingdom of God is nigh. Verily I say unto you, This generation shall not pass away, till all things be accomplished. Heaven and earth shall pass away: but my words shall not pass away. But take heed to yourselves, lest haply your hearts be overcharged with surfeiting, and drunkenness, and cares of this life, and that day come on you suddenly as a snare: for so shall it come upon all them that dwell on the face of all the earth. But watch ye at every season, making supplication, that ye may prevail to escape all these things that shall come to pass, and to stand before the Son of man.

LUKE 21:25-36

Chapter Four

Whence This Longing?

EVERY generation of Christians has carried the signs of Christ's second coming in its own bosom. "Who shall deliver me" is the perennial cry of men awakened to their own sinfulness within and aware of the world's wickedness without. The newness of life which they have found individually in Christ expands into the flaming hope that all existence shall one day receive deliverance from the thralldom of sin, and be ushered into a "new heaven and a new earth." This irrepressible hope they find confirmed in the promises of Scripture, until they see all creation groaning and travailing, longing and yearning, for that day. It is a glorious prospect, a great unfolding epic. The really splendid epochs of the Church's life have always been those in which the believers have thrilled to the glad knowledge that He was coming soon.

At first thought, it seems a dismal prospect.

Why wish this intriguing world of skyscrapers and technicolor films to end? It may have been all right for the early church to yearn for an end to its kind of world, with its leprosy, famine and Nero's arena. But with our jet planes and sulfa drugs, why should we want to exchange our age for something we have never seen up there in the sky? We are willing to have this one doctored up a bit to eliminate wars and unemployment and cancer, but we are not sure that we would want to trade it in for something quite new.

Christ recognized this pitfall. Our hearts may be overcharged with surfeiting. The very abundance of things, and our attachment for them, could very well snuff out any longing for His return. We are children both of time and of eternity. Our real citizenship as Christians is in His Kingdom. Of necessity we are dwellers for a few fleeting years on this earth. But this is not our native land. The fearful tragedy lies in man, destined for the eternal Kingdom, becoming content with life on the earth. We may be satisfied to live as highly complex animals who think, and talk, and compose symphonies, but as animals still. Nor do we need carpeted homes and Cadillac cars to face this temptation. The barefoot sharecropper may be as insensible to the eternal, invisible Kingdom as the bejewelled debutante. The sublime pantheism of a Walden Pond may be as blinded to this world's haunting impoverishment as the soggy and crass materialism of a Babbitt.

Another hazard to the longing is some false escape, such as drunkenness. Confronted with the utter failure of this world to satisfy, we seek respite or surcease in one of many detours. The annual eight-billion-dollar liquor bill in the United States is stark evidence of man's inability to cope with life's frustrations. Life cheats him and pummels him, and he runs away. That is what the British colonial did at a bar in Calcutta. When a friend warned him that he was drinking too much, he lifted his filled glass, drained it in a gulp, and replied, "My dear sir, this is the speediest passage out of India." Others may choose more refined routes, such as taking a trip to forget; or distorting the facts of life to gloss over unpleasant things and remember only the pleasant. Still others end up in dementia praecox and find piteous escape from grim reality in some asylum. Man, face to face with the abysmal insolvency of this world's bank, easily slips into some false path of escape.

Even if he does not run away, he may wander aimlessly about among the cares and anxieties of life, and not be caught up and find the release of an eternal longing. Christ cautioned that the cares of life, like weeds, could choke the divine word in man's heart. Satan has a subtile way of representing worry as a virtue. The mother who worries must, therefore, be a good mother; the senator who worries must be a good senator. But worry is not the same as a genuine Christian concern or anxiety. In that magnificent discourse called the Sermon on the Mount, Jesus warns against fretting and worry by pointing to God's care of grass and lilies and sparrows, and then goes on to tell

what area should be our real concern, "Seek ye
first his kingdom and his righteousness. . . ."
Instead of bank balances and tomorrow's market,
we are to have prior concern for the inner Kingdom, our own relationship to it and its relevance
to the affairs of men. We are to lose our lives, and
with them our cares, in a supreme loyalty to Him.
To worry is to sin in distrust or feeble faith. And
worries, like little buzzing insects, may divert us
from lifting our eyes to the eternal hills from
whence our help could come.

A Christian's longing for deliverance from this
world's wretchedness roots in his own inner wickedness. It is the great chasm between what he
himself is and what he ought to be that creates
his discontent. The sin in the world around him
disturbs him, to be sure; but his despair lies in
his own sin. Paul's longing for Christ's return and
the eternal emancipation of that event came not
from being buffeted about by an evil world, but
welled forth from a desire to be rid of his own
inner wretchedness. The cleavage in his own bosom, the failures of his own will, the lust in his
own heart, prompted his passion. Satan is quite
willing to have a man long for Christ's return if
the longing be prompted by a desire to be rid of
his neighbor's wickedness instead of his own. And
often this magnificent expectancy for Christ's
coming gets twisted into being primarily a dis-
gust with our world and not with ourselves. The
wars of nations, not the warring in our own
hearts, trouble us. The corruption in government
and business, not our own inner corruption, dis-

tresses us. It is the money squandered by our neighbors that is bad, not the money hoarded in our own bank accounts or reinvested into ever-expanding holdings. With pious vindictiveness we threaten this wicked world with Christ's return, blindly confident that on that day all our sinful associates will get their just dues, and we will stride proudly by the pit, up the slopes to celestial bliss.

It is not so with the man who, alone before his God, has cried, "O wretched man that I am. . . ." The Holy Spirit has opened his eyes to see himself as a poor, lost and condemned creature. The utter disparity between his own life and the life which God's holy law demands strikes him with shattering force. The overt evil of his thoughts, desires, words, and deeds crowds in upon his conscience. The good he might have done but neglected to do hovers over him like a ghost. He finds no rest. He cannot find comfort by comparing himself to others, as he so often has done, because He is alone before God, and "others" are not there. Like David, he felt God's hand of judgment day and night; like Isaiah, he knows that he is undone. His anguish is the sinner's sorrow over sin. Not sin's inevitable hangover, but sin itself, becomes his pain. There is no wretchedness so torturous as an unforgiven soul cornered before the judgment of God. From this there is no earthly release. To try squirming out by good works only entangles the soul the more in deceit, disillusion, and despair. There is no help, save help from the outside. Then comes the tender and strong voice of the Savior, "Behold, I stand at the door and knock." Redemption is nigh, on the very threshold. And the soul that ceases its striving falls into the gentle embrace of Christ's forgiving grace. The grim condemnation of the law is no more, life's fierce restlessness gives way to a strange peace, and the heart leaps for joy in a new freedom. He has been delivered. The fingers of the soul, feeling furtively so long for something to hold to, grasp the promises which are more fixed than heaven and earth.

This drama of deliverance, enacted in millions of redeemed in every century, has its cosmic counterpart in Christ's second coming. This world itself, in the anarchy of sin's rebellion, will one day yield its slavery to the King of Kings. Sin's dominion, as well as its guilt, will be crushed. This fallen world will be no more. The Redeemer who came to Bethlehem as a lowly servant will then be fully revealed as the Judge of the living and the dead; and all flesh, redeemed and unredeemed, will behold His glory.

It is for us today to make sure that were that day to come tomorrow we would be among the redeemed. If today we live in the Kingdom of His grace, then tomorrow will but usher us into the wider spaces of the Kingdom of His glory. Jesus invites us to stop our fruitless searchings for contentment among this world's deceiving resources, to cease our own vain strivings for peace, and to yield ourselves to full dependence upon His grace.

Our age is weighed down by the heavy pall of

impending doom. Our mechanical ingenuity has turned traitor and her children are threatening unparalleled devastation. Men sleep feverishly before the specter of a thousand Hiroshimas. Time has assumed a dreadful urgency. In Omar Khayyam's words,

> The bird of time has but a little way to flutter,
> And the bird is on the wing.

In the first century Paul, too, lived feverishly under the consciousness that time was ebbing fast away. But his intuition was the urgency of God's Spirit. This world had its impermanence, not because of its bombs, but because of God's judgment upon its sins. The patience of God could not endure forever. And as He gave deliverance from the guilt and dominion of sin to every man willing to receive it, as He ushered man, one by one, into the glorious liberty of the Gospel, so one day He would consummate existence itself, and put an end to the anguish rampant in a fallen world.

Whether this world shall go on one day, one year, or a thousand millenniums more, there still is no time to lose. Your day may soon be over. He who said, "I must work the works of him who sent me while it is day" expects us, His followers, to follow Him in work too. There are a thousand honorable daily tasks to be done faithfully and well. He Himself worked as a carpenter. There are families to be reared in the fear of the Lord. There are churches to be built and maintained. Above all, there are people, hundreds of millions of them, to be reached with the glorious tidings of deliverance and salvation. To know that He is coming soon intensifies every duty, ennobles every task, and hastens every mission. And as we set to work, we must be vigilant, ever on watch and constant in prayer, that we reach that day standing among the hosts arrayed before the great white throne.

Forgive us, O Father, for living as if this life and this world were never to end. Enable us to live each day as if Christ on the morrow were to come. And when He does come, grant that we may be found standing expectantly before Him eagerly awaiting the fullness of His glory. Prepare these days the hearts of thy Church for another blessed Festival of Advent. In Jesus' Name we pray.

AMEN

Let your loins be girded about, and your lamps burning; and be ye yourselves like unto men looking for their lord, when he shall return from the marriage feast; that, when he cometh and knocketh, they may straightway open unto him. Blessed are those servants, whom the lord when he cometh shall find watching: verily I say unto you, that he shall gird himself, and make them sit down to meat, and shall come and serve them. And if he shall come in the second watch, and if in the third, and find them so, blessed are those servants. But know this, that if the master of the house had known in what hour the thief was coming, he would have watched, and not have left his house to be broken through. Be ye also ready: for in an hour that ye think not the Son of man cometh.

LUKE 12:35-40

Chapter Five

The Son of Man Cometh

THE Son of Man cometh. These words summarize a truth that is one of the greatest and most distinctive in all Scripture. If this be truth from God, then man has a solid rock upon which to base anticipation, expectation, and hope. But here also God pronounces a judgment upon all human power and achievement. These words hold out only fear and despair for the one who has not allowed Christ a place in his life.

There are various ways in which Christ comes to men. He first made His appearance in far-off Bethlehem on Christmas night. A choir of angels sang a never-repeated hallelujah chorus to mark that event. During those three marvelous years when He walked among men, He came with divine power and grace to communities, towns, and the hearts of men. Whenever and wherever He came the lives of men were different. There were those who were driven farther from God and deeper into sin because of the judgment brought by His word and life. Others were driven to repentance by that same judgment and found in Him healing and comfort and life.

Through all these twenty centuries since Christ died, He has continued to "come." Death did not change His essence, but only altered the manner of His speaking and working. Wherever there has been the gospel, God's unchanging Word; wherever the Sacraments He established have been faithfully administered, there Christ has come. In an unseen, though powerful manner, each new generation of men has known the reality of His presence. In every age there have been those who turned against Him. It could not be otherwise, for His word and life bring men to judgment and condemnation. But always there have been others who have found peace and life because of the reality of His coming.

The Christ of judgment comes to men, too, through events that occur in the lives of men and of groups. The Word speaks of days of visitation. Men travel a journey of their own choosing with little or no visible evidence of the restraining or guiding hand of God. They are free to choose their course in private or group life. But then come days when the power of God manifests itself and men face the consequence of their choices. Every crop that is planted matures and develops in preparation for the time of harvest. Every planting in men's lives too has its time of harvest. Our generation has seen the coming of Christ in the destruction of arrogant world powers, in the destruction of systems, and in the blessing of God upon those who choose the way of obedience to Him. "Whatsoever a man soweth, that shall he also reap."

But still another "coming" of Christ lies ahead. The Word of God goes farther than we have thus far gone in pointing to Him who said of Himself, "The Son of Man cometh." This He had in mind when He said, "I will see you again." The prophetic vision of this other coming was before His eye when He spoke these words, "When the Son of Man shall come in his glory, and all the angels with him, then shall he sit on the throne of his glory: and before him shall be gathered all the nations." Language such as this looks beyond the coming of Christ in Word and Sacrament and sees something other than the guiding control of historic events. Once again the eternal Christ may be expected to break into history in a manner that transcends the ordinary nature of historic cause and effect.

Connected with His coming are other events which belong to the revelation of Scripture. At the time of His coming will occur the resurrection of the dead. "All that are in the graves shall hear his voice and shall come forth." This will be the time of judgment. All men will be called into the presence of God and held accountable for the lives they have lived. "Neither doth the Father judge any man, but he hath given all judgment unto the Son." "He shall set the sheep on his right hand, but the goats on the left." Connected with that coming is the promise of the transformation of the present order. Righteousness will have its reward, sin will be eliminated, and God will rule His people in a glorious Kingdom of righteousness. Both Old and New Testament writers rise to sublime heights as they picture the glories of that great day of God. Peter describes it so, "The heavens shall pass away with a great noise, and the elements shall be dissolved with fervent heat, and the earth and the works that are therein shall be burned up." In one of the most beautiful and comforting passages of the New Testament John sees "a new heaven and a new earth: for the first heaven and the first earth are passed away."

How many sorrowing, bewildered souls have thrilled to the prospect of the day when God "shall wipe away every tear from their eyes; and death shall be no more; neither shall there be mourning, nor crying, nor pain, any more: the first things are passed away." In a day when men look forward with fear and dread to the day when another war threatens to destroy civilization, Scripture pictures the day when Christ will come again. For when "the Son of Man cometh," Isaiah says of Him, "He will judge between the nations, and will decide concerning many peoples; and they shall beat their swords into plowshares, and their spears into pruning-hooks; nation shall not lift up sword against nation, neither shall they learn war any more."

"The Son of Man cometh." Today He comes humbly, begging men to accept His gift of life. In that day "every knee shall bow and every tongue confess that Jesus Christ is Lord." Now He is invisible, living and ruling in the hearts of men, exerting Himself through a Word that is often despised and unimpressive. But in the great day of the Lord there will be the glory of the angels and a Word that compels all men to recognize its power. In our day men often hide their inmost hearts and wickedness appears to be in the saddle. In that day the secrets of men will be revealed and both good and evil will receive their just rewards.

No truth of Scripture is more plain, no promise more definite than that concerning which we are speaking. The band of disciples, so broken and downhearted beneath the cross, those friends who watched Him leave the Mount of Olives, found their inspiration in the hope of His return. So plainly and unmistakably had Jesus taught them this that they lived in eager anticipation of that great day. Persecution and suffering could be borne, for soon He would return to release them. The attractions of a sinful world held little appeal, for in a little while their trusted Friend would return to escort them in glory to the heavenly home. What if wicked men and enemies of the cross appeared to hold the upper hand? Soon the powerful Son of God would come and they would face their day of judgment. In glorious language, word piles upon word and phrase upon phrase in the effort to express their exaltation as they look forward to the day of His appearing.

It is strange that so glorious and plain a truth should sometimes during the centuries have lost its grip on men. At times it has come into serious disrepute. Too often it has become only a phrase in a credal statement or something to be explained away lest it offend minds who pride themselves upon their rejection of anything supernatural.

Part of the reason for our failure to live in this truth lies in the years of waiting. Year after year, decade after decade, century after century has passed. Sixty-five generations have come and gone. Nineteen hundred years of life have crossed the stage of history. Still, Christ has not come. How very natural, then, for each new generation to feel it is to be denied the privilege of personally greeting His appearing! How altogether human to postpone it so far into the future that it becomes virtually meaningless!

Perhaps, too, we have lost some of our faith in it because of the misguided zeal and un-Biblical teaching of a few who themselves love Christ. Such have ventured to intrude upon the hidden counsels of God. They have made themselves and God's truth ridiculous by fantastic predictions concerning the Lord's return. Forgotten have been such words as these: "In an hour ye think not," "As a thief in the night," and "Of that day and hour knoweth no one, not even the angels of heaven, neither the Son, but the Father only."

We must be very careful lest the delay in His coming, or the ill-advised teachings of fanatics, or our own natural reluctance about believing what lies outside our experience blind our eyes to this glorious promise of God's Word.

Our day needs a revitalization of its faith in the Christ who "cometh." Ours is a time of discouragement and of fear. The mood of this post-war period is one of uncertainty, and of cynicism, and of doubt. Modern man has been matured in an atmosphere filled with talk of progress and of promises of what man may achieve. He has breathed the air of Greek faith in the inherent goodness of man and the ability of man to win his way forward to the good life. He has been encouraged in the idea that about him and within him are natural forces which are gradually leading mankind to higher levels. Then comes an experience such as we now are passing through. Civilized men, men who have been trained in centuries of Christian teaching, embrace a barbarism as hideous as that of a thousand years ago. On every hand appear the evidences of demonic forces so powerful that the entire human race seems helpless in their grasp. Unloosed in every land, among victor and vanquished alike, are evil powers which degrade mankind and upset every possible concept of goodness and right. No wonder modern man stands bewildered and aghast in the midst of the wreckage of such a day.

None of this is strange to the reader of God's Word. It has always held that man is inherently evil and that the world is filled with powers too strong for human strength to overcome. It holds out the promise of a victory over evil if men will permit the power of God to come into their lives. But on every page is written the awful truth that man in his blindness will not seek that power.

Confident and arrogant in his own abilities, he sees no need of accepting the life that God freely offers to him. Always there is a remnant within mankind that knows the power of God, but the masses of men live on without Him. Facing such a world with awful realism, Scripture sees no hope for man except in the return of Jesus Christ. Individual men know victory in Christ in anticipation of His coming. Groups here and there approach such victory. But the real victory of God is bound up in the one who cometh, and in the day of His appearing. Scripture holds no promise short of that.

It is for the events of such a day that God admonishes us to be ready. "Be ye also ready, for in an hour ye think not, the Son of Man cometh." Such preparation or readiness is no different from that which must characterize each day one lives. No special exercise or spiritual exaltation is required. The preparation for death or for the coming of Christ is the preparation for Christmas or for tomorrow. The figure used is that of one who binds his clothing about him so that nothing hinders freedom of action and movement. No attachments bind one that must be broken off when He comes. The adjustments and the corrections which life requires are cared for. The one who is ready is the one who daily lays aside his sin, has made all things right with his neighbor and can leave at a moment's notice.

Here is judgment upon the modern skeptic who is unwilling to commit himself to any faith. Here is a judgment upon those who maintain attachment to a sinful world while claiming to be Christians. Here is a judgment on all who are bound up in their own ambitions and plans and desires.

In simple but terrible language, Scripture pictures that great day.

And the kings of the earth, and the great men, and the rich men, and the chief captains, and the mighty men, and every bondman, and every free man, hid themselves in the dens and in the rocks of the mountains; And said to the mountains and rocks, Fall on us, and hide us from the face of him that sitteth on the throne, and from the wrath of the Lamb: For the great day of his wrath is come; and who shall be able to stand?

REV. 6:15-17

But by way of contrast:

Blessed are those servants, whom the Lord when he cometh shall find watching: verily I say unto you, that he shall gird himself, and make them to sit down to meat, and will come forth and serve them.

LUKE 12:37

AMEN

And being asked by the Pharisees, when the kingdom of God cometh, he answered them and said, The kingdom of God cometh not with observation: neither shall they say, Lo, here! or, There! for lo, the kingdom of God is within you. And he said unto the disciples, The days will come, when ye shall desire to see one of the days of the Son of man, and ye shall not see it. And they shall say to you, Lo, there! Lo, here! go not away, nor follow after them: for as the lightning, when it lighteneth out of the one part under the heaven, shineth unto the other part under heaven; so shall the Son of man be in his day. But first must he suffer many things and be rejected of this generation. And as it came to pass in the days of Noah, even so shall it be also in the days of the Son of man. They ate, they drank, they married, they were given in marriage, until the day that Noah entered into the ark, and the flood came, and destroyed them all. Likewise even as it came to pass in the days of Lot; they ate, they drank, they bought, they sold, they planted, they builded; but in the day that Lot went out from Sodom it rained fire and brimstone from heaven, and destroyed them all: after the same manner shall it be in the day that the Son of man is revealed.

LUKE 17:20-30

Chapter Six

Thy Kingdom Come

MEN cannot become like God unless they look at God. We cannot become Christ-like unless we consider Christ. Earth cannot become like heaven if men never look to heaven. Prayers for a better world do not reach their most sublime height until we pray *Thy Kingdom come*. Men will not learn to live heaven-patterned lives until they learn that we are "sojourners" here on earth, and our destination is heaven, and that there is a vital relation between the destination and the direction. If our destination is to be heaven then our walk must be heavenward. If we hope for the heavenly glory, our eyes must be fixed on "the things above." If in this perplexing life we want help from heaven, we must "lift our eyes unto the hills" from whence comes our help. If our goal is the City of God, where the "Lord God Almighty and the Lamb are the temple of it," we must take out our first citizenship papers and en-

ter the forecourts of the City here and now. We
have not learned to pray until with lifted eyes
and longing heart we have breathed the Advent
prayer, "Thy Kingdom come."

Men who would pray that prayer must (1)
have a concern for the Kingdom, (2) know the
nature of the Kingdom, (3) look for the consummation of the Kingdom.

Concern about the Kingdom

When the Pharisees came to Jesus asking when
the Kingdom of God should come, they at least
showed an interest, even a deep concern, about the
Kingdom. For generations the Jews had been
brought up in the expectation of the coming of
the Messiah. Had not the Prophets down through
the centuries promised them that the Messiah
would come, the Anointed One of God, the Savior
and King of Israel?

But as the tradition grew, the Jewish conception of the Messiah grew far beyond anything the
Prophets had declared. And when the fullness of
time was about to dawn they had come to expect
a Messiah far different from the humble Savior
Zechariah had promised, when he said: "Rejoice
greatly, O daughter of Zion; shout, O daughter
of Jerusalem; behold thy King cometh unto thee:
he is just, and having salvation; lowly, and riding
upon an ass, and upon a colt the foal of an ass."
Now the Jews, under the ambitious leadership of
the Pharisees, were looking for a worldly king, a
conquering hero, who should crush the Roman
tyrant and all the enemies who had so long op-

pressed them. He would set up a Jewish kingdom which would outshine all other kingdoms in majesty and in power. The noble spiritual conception of Zechariah had given way to a worldly, materialistic idea of the Kingdom of God.

With that conception in their warped minds we can understand why the Pharisees were interested enough to ask Jesus when the Kingdom of God should come. It was a purely selfish question. For when the Messiah appeared and set up His Kingdom, they, as the religious leaders of the people, would most certainly sit in the highest councils of the King. It was the kind of question Herod put to his chief priests when he asked them "where Christ should be born."

Today who cares about the Kingdom of God? Man is god. Science is king. And materialism is his religion. A millennium and a half ago the "best seller" was *The City of God*. Today the average "best seller" is a lurid picture of the depths to which man can fall. A thousand years ago the finest collection of art in the world would be almost exclusively religious, yes, Christian. Today you can attend art exhibitions from coast to coast and search in vain for one religious picture. Speaking at the president's inauguration at the University of Minnesota recently, President Shuster of Hunter College made the startling but ominous statement that man through scientific atomic research had risen to such heights that he had arrived almost at creation. But, he added with awesome soberness, he has only succeeded in unmasking man.

There are, however, even today men like the Pharisees who are asking about the Kingdom of God. There are books being written, both fiction and non-fiction, with titles that reflect an interest in the Kingdom. We call to mind *The Keys of the Kingdom, Is the Kingdom of God Realism?* and similar titles. But even in church circles how much talk is there about the Kingdom of God, when it will come, when Christ will return? And when men do talk about it, how confused is often their idea of what the Kingdom of God is.

The unbelieving world dares sometimes to talk about the Kingdom of God. By it she usually means an era of peace and prosperity arrived at through a one-world economy, free trade, international currency, international control of atomic energy, all held together by a United Nations organization. And, some would add, all dominated by the philosophy of Karl Marx.

A large section of the Christian Church talks about the Kingdom of God and means the Roman Catholic Church. On the other hand there is Modernist Protestantism whose Kingdom is an earthly Utopia which men can usher in by moral rearmament, good living, and social legislation.

All three of these pray in one way or another, "Thy Kingdom come." The first prays it with blaspheming lips, not to God but to man, and proceeds to lift itself by its own bootstraps. The second prays it and adds, "Make all men Roman Catholics." The third supplements the prayer with, "Give us time and we'll figure it out for ourselves, maybe pass a law."

Jesus answers all three, "The Kingdom of God cometh not with observation." The Kingdom is not here just because the world is at peace and crops are abundant. It may be simply post-war exhaustion, or the breathless calm before the next storm. The Kingdom will not come when you have succeeded in squeezing all men into one organized church. The Kingdom is not about to dawn just because the world has reached the highest peak of scientific knowledge, of social security, and of international cooperation. In all three there is a fundamental misunderstanding of the nature of the Kingdom of God.

The Nature of the Kingdom

"The Kingdom of God cometh not with observation." You can't see it. You can't put your finger on it. It isn't a material, outward organization. It isn't a theocracy ruled over by John Calvin or the Pope at Rome. You can't bring it in by social reform or legislation. You can pass laws outlawing prostitution, prohibiting strong drink, forbidding juvenile delinquency, punishing crime with death. But that does not bring in the Kingdom. All the efforts of men—even of good men—can never establish the Kingdom of God. For it is a creation of God. "It is your Father's good pleasure to *give* you the Kingdom," said Jesus to His disciples on a previous occasion. And now He adds significantly, "The Kingdom of God is within you." It is a hidden, invisible, intangible thing. And yet it is a *real* thing, living among men and in the hearts of men.

It is a spiritual Kingdom, a Kingdom of hearts. Citizenship is by faith in Jesus Christ. On the throne is the King of Kings. Not only King of the Jews, or King of the Gentiles, but for all men King of Righteousness and King of Love. And such is His Kingdom among men, a Kingdom of righteousness and love. For all who are members of His Kingdom by faith in Him live in righteousness, governed and motivated by only one law, the Law of Love. The love of God manifested in the Cross of Calvary has power not only to save men from their sins. It has power for good, unselfish, healthy, Christlike living. Lloyd Douglas has brought it out beautifully in *The Robe,* where he depicts Marcellus, the Roman Centurion, as not only redeemed by the Cross but living by it through fiery persecution until he dies a martyr.

All who live the good life by faith are members of the Kingdom. It is a matter of the heart, a personal, single-minded allegiance to the King. So intimate is the relationship that a Christian says with Paul, "I am crucified with Christ: Nevertheless I live; yet not I, but Christ liveth in me; and the life which I now live in the flesh, I live by the faith of the Son of God, who loved me and gave himself for me." By the power of Christ I live *in* the world, but am not *of* the world. I am a citizen of the United States of America, but as a citizen of the Kingdom of God I owe my highest allegiance to the King of Kings. Peter and the other Apostles were loyal Roman citizens, but when they were ordered to cease preaching Christ, they said, "We ought to obey God rather than men."

This Kingdom is the Church of Jesus Christ. Here again the words of Jesus must be remembered, that "the Kingdom of God cometh not with observation." It is not this church or that church. For "the Kingdom of God is within you." The Church of Christ is not an organization. It is a fellowship of those who believe in Christ, scattered throughout the world and through all Christian churches. So intimate is the fellowship with Christ and with one another in the Church that St. Paul says, it is "the Body of Christ."

This fellowship of believers in Christ is held together by the Holy Spirit through the Word of God and the Sacraments. By the Gospel of the crucified and risen Christ, given us in Word and Sacrament, the Spirit creates and maintains life in His Church and her members. We sense the life of Christ Himself pulsating in us when we gather with other Christians to worship Him, to receive His life-giving Word, and to partake of His Body and Blood in the blessed Sacrament. Breathless and believing the Church gathers in Holy Communion, and with all the saints we pray,

O most merciful God, grant me to receive the Body of Thine Only-begotten Son, our Lord Jesus Christ, which He took of the Virgin Mary, that I may be found worthy to be incorporated into His mystical Body, and accounted among His members.

Bearing one another's burdens we pray in the unity of the Body of Christ the ancient prayer of the Church:

Vouchsafe, O Lord, to behold the tribulations of the people, the perils of the nations, the groans of prisoners, the miseries of orphans, the necessities of strangers, the helplessness of the weak, the depression of the weary, the infirmities of the aged, the aspirations of the young, the vows of virgins, the lamentations of widows.

This is "the Holy Christian Church, the Communion of Saints," in which we believe. And as often as we rise from this "Feast of Forgiveness," our glad hearts are singing with new strength and purpose,

Now lettest Thou Thy guest depart
With full assurance in his heart;
For such communion, Lord, with Thee
May a new life my offering be.

Thus, as the hymn-writer says, our life in the Kingdom of God is a *new* life. The gracious Spirit who brought us into that life in holy Baptism now sustains and renews the life in us day by day through Word and Sacrament. We get a new perspective in life. We are now enabled to look beyond the material and tangible things to the spiritual and eternal. We aren't driven into a stone wall of despair by suffering and misfortune; for by faith we look beyond to His promise that "all things work together for good to them that love God." "The fellowship of his sufferings" goes hand in hand with the "power of his resurrection." We no longer make a prison for ourselves by focusing our attention and our affections on things present. We lift longing eyes of faith and with joyous anticipation we wait for the consummation of the Kingdom.

The Consummation of the Kingdom

Christ is coming again! Turning from the Pharisees to His disciples, He gives to them and to us a precious word of warning and comfort. There will be hard days ahead, days of suffering and great tribution for His followers, times when they will cry, "Lord, how long?" The days will come, says Jesus, "when ye shall desire to see one of the days of the Son of man, and ye shall not see it." So serious is the testing of the faith of the children of the Kingdom. In the midst of sore trials Jesus does not permit them to have a glimpse of the glory which is awaiting them. Their faith in Him and in His promise must suffice. Instead there will come to the suffering Christian false prophets and teachers who presume to prophesy when Christ will come. "See here; or, see there." From its earliest history the Church has been heckled and torn by these fanatical leeches, who by twisting prophecy have dared to announce the day and hour of His coming. Charles T. Russell, father of the so-called Russellites, or Jehovah's Witnesses, threw together a number of unrelated Bible passages and proclaimed that the end of the world would come in 1914. Christ would return then. It didn't happen in 1914, so he changed his calculations and announced the end for 1925. He weakened, however, and in 1920 adopted a more cautious slogan, "Millions now living will never die." We can find his salesmen on the busiest corner of every big city, selling faithfully the propaganda sheet of this benighted sect, *The Watch Tower*. There are hundreds of stories circulating about

the families of "the faithful" who sold all they had
and climbed up on the roof to await the coming
of the millennium.

Jesus warns His Church of these false teachers
and says, "Go not after them, nor follow them."
The return of Christ is not going to be according to any of the best laid plans of men. He will
not come when men expect Him; but "as a thief
in the night" comes, so unexpected will be His
coming. The world will be going about its business, as it did in the days of Noah and of Lot.
Noah knew the deluge would come, because he
believed the word of Jehovah. Every stroke of his
hammer on that ark was a call to repentance. But
people only laughed at him and went back to
their eating and drinking and merrymaking, with
no thought of death or judgment or God. Into
that life of godless self-sufficiency crashed the flood
of doom. God is not mocked.

It was the same kind of world in Lot's day. It
is the same kind of world today. Men spend
their time eating and drinking, buying and selling, planting and building. The prophets of God
are pounding out the ark of salvation, calling people to repent and believe the Gospel. Every sermon, every testimony to Christ, every tolling of a
church bell is a stroke of Noah's hammer, ticking
off the minutes, the hours, the days, until the
heavenly trumpet shall sound the return of Christ
"to judge the quick and the dead."

Christ will surely come. He will come when
God has made all things ready. Jesus told the disciples that He must first "suffer many things."

Here is the first great step in the carrying out of God's plan for saving the world. Only by the blood of the Son of God can such a world as Noah saw, as Lot saw, as we see today, be redeemed from the eternal misery of sin. Noah and Lot pointed their "lost generation" forward to the Cross. The Church today points our "lost generation" backward to the same Cross. Nothing else can save them. But Christ can. He died that they might live. He lives that they may not die forever in hell. Will our materialistic and pleasure-loving generation reject Him as they did in the days of Noah and of Lot and even in the days of His incarnation?

All the while the Church is proclaiming to all the world this saving Gospel of a crucified and risen Christ, she waits patiently for His return. He has promised that He will surely come to gather His own, the living and the dead, into His Kingdom of glory. He has promised to sustain us till He comes. "In the world ye shall have tribulation: but be of good cheer; I have overcome the world." "Let not your heart be troubled. . . . Peace I leave with you, my peace I give unto you: not as the world giveth, give I unto you. Let not your heart be troubled, neither let it be afraid." "Lo, I am with you alway, even unto the end of the world."

The Church of Christ lives as in the eleventh hour. In breathless anticipation of His glorious coming she goes joyfully about her redemptive task, her eyes lifted to the hills. Within the heart of her every member two great loves are beating, the love of Christ and the love of men. In reality they are only *one* love, the love of Christ. For while the love of Christ pulls him heavenward and creates a longing to be free from this world of cares and pain, and to be with Christ, the same love of Christ drives him to men, to bring them Christ, the glory of His fellowship on earth, the joy of His salvation, the peace of forgiveness of sins, the glorious hope of life everlasting. It drives him further out of his shell of self-sufficiency and complacency into the unhappy world where men are suffering, weeping, fighting, killing. Into that unhappy humanity he can come with the only remedy, the only consolation, the only hope. For he has Christ, the Friend of sinners, the Prince of peace, the Savior of the world.

Advent 1946! The world is in the grip of fear. But as men read the headlines and tremble, and listen to the screaming radio and go mad, the Christian Church goes calmly about her business saying, "Thy will be done on earth, as it is in heaven." And lifting her eyes above the atomic cloud she prays in faith, "Thy Kingdom come." Out of heaven comes the sure answer of the Son of God, "The gates of hell shall not prevail against my Church."

Surely I come quickly.
Amen. Even so, come, Lord Jesus.

AMEN

Now when John heard in the prison the works of the Christ, he sent by his disciples and said unto him, Art thou he that cometh, or look we for another? And Jesus answered and said unto them, Go and tell John the things which ye hear and see: the blind receive their sight, and the lame walk, the lepers are cleansed, and the deaf hear, and the dead are raised up, and the poor have good tidings preached to them. And blessed is he, whosoever shall find no occasion of stumbling in me. And as these went their way, Jesus began to say unto the multitudes concerning John, What went ye out into the wilderness to behold? a reed shaken with the wind? But what went ye out to see? a man clothed in soft raiment? Behold, they that wear soft raiment are in kings' houses. But wherefore went ye out? to see a prophet? Yea, I say unto you, and much more than a prophet. This is he, of whom it is written, Behold, I send my messenger before thy face, who shall prepare thy way before thee.

MATTHEW 11:2-10

Chapter Seven

Art Thou He That Cometh?

JOHN, the forerunner of Jesus, must have been a striking figure. Though our knowledge of him is very limited, the few facts we do possess reveal him as a strong, vigorous personality. His attire and diet were simple. No doubt this outdoor life gave him a rugged, healthy exterior. His manner of speech was direct and convincing, filled with the wisdom of the soil and the ways of the common people. He was a fearless man who dared to expose the sins of the people. He was on the side of the poor, the distressed, and the needy.

His voice thundered in the streets of Jerusalem and echoed in the halls of the king's palace. It was to be expected that his denunciation of the king's marriage would reach the ears of the ruling pair and bring down upon John the wrath of King Herod. Like the ancient prophet, Nathan, so John pointed his finger at the king. He said of the marriage, "It is not lawful." The fury of licentious

Herodias and cowardly Herod descended on John, and he was cast into prison.

Here was a man whose only enclosure heretofore had been the canopy of heaven and the distant horizon. Now he was confined to the four walls of a dungeon. He was a young man at the height of his strength physically and mentally. Jesus paid him this high tribute, "Among them that are born of women, there hath not risen a greater than John the Baptist." In spite of his genius and youth John languished in prison. A thousand tormenting thoughts must have crowded into his mind. Was God just? Did He care more for Herod than for one of His own honest prophets? How could a wise and just God tolerate such a man as Herod and allow one of His own to be imprisoned?

The greatest strain on his faith, however, was the rising tide of doubt in his mind regarding the Messiahship of Jesus. Vividly John must have recalled that glorious day in his ministry when he baptized the young man Jesus of Nazareth, and a voice from heaven said, "This is my beloved Son in whom I am well pleased." Now, while wasting away in prison, he thought over the past events. He thought of the day when he had singled out Jesus and had pointed Him out as the long-awaited Messiah. Had he been mistaken? Was this the Chosen One of Israel? Was this the eternal Son of God who was to save His people from their sins? John thought, wondered, and doubted. Bits of news filtered into the prison, but they were not completely reassuring—mostly small half-

truths which are so often carried to us by people
who are careless with the truth. John had doubts
about the Messiahship of Jesus. Indeed, John may
have thought that Jesus should have come to him
there in prison and by some miraculous means
broken down the walls and freed the fearless
prophet of God.

Finally John could stand it no longer. He sent
a friend of his to investigate, to put directly to
Jesus this question: "Art thou he that cometh,
or look we for another?"

The question revealed the doubt that was on
the mind of John. The question also revealed the
greatness of John the Baptist. There was no har-
anguing. There was no scolding. There was no
complaining. He merely asked a direct question,
"Art thou he that cometh, or look we for another?" He was an honest man who refused to
draw conclusions until he had the facts and first-
hand information. John may have entertained
several incorrect conceptions as to what the Messiah should be like, but he was willing to hear the
truth and be corrected.

Too many of us seem to press Jesus into a pre-
conceived conception as to what He should be
like. Therefore, when we come face to face with
Christ, we fail to recognize Him or refuse to accept Him.

The answer which Jesus gave to John was also
direct and simple: "Go tell John all the things
that you hear and see." He did not reprimand
John for his viewpoint. He recognized the right
of the Prophet of the Wilderness to ask questions,

to search for the truth. There was no quoting of the prophets or giving a long genealogy. There was no attempt to force John into a truth.

"Go tell John," said Jesus, "the things you hear and see. The blind receive their sight, and the lame walk, the lepers are healed, and the deaf hear, the dead are raised up, and the poor have the Gospel preached to them. And blessed is he who findeth no occasion of stumbling in me." In other words Jesus said to them, "Go tell John the facts. Present the well-known evidence. Let him use his own judgment on the evidence as the Holy Spirit guides him in their evaluation. The blind receive their sight, and the lame walk, the lepers are healed, and the deaf hear, the dead are raised up, and the poor have the Gospel preached to them."

It was Jesus who said, "By their fruits ye shall know them," and He was willing to have His own ministry tested by the same standard. "John," He was saying, "my ministry may not be exactly as you thought it should be, but the evidence that can be brought to you in the prison of the results of my preaching will be sufficient for a man of your heart and mind to assure you that I am the eternal Son of God."

The world in which Jesus lived was vastly different from our own. The more obvious differences lie in the field of transportation and communication. The slow-moving caravan wending its way across the desert waste-land of Palestine is astonishing contrast to the atomic power, jet-propulsion age in which we are living. Today the church bell of Bethlehem at Christmastime can be heard around the earth. In the time of Jesus the only sounding board to the human voice was a mountainside or the quiet surface of a lake. Though much of the world today lives as the people lived in the time of Jesus, civilization at the forefront is vastly different.

However, the more important differences are to be found in the care of the needy, the suffering, and those who live in fear of darkness. To visualize the difference try to imagine, if you will, what would happen if in any one of our large cities all the hospitals were closed and the sick emptied out upon the streets; if the crippled, the maimed, the halt, the blind, and the deaf were forced to earn their living by begging on the street corners; if every disease-tormented person were to have all our modern means of fighting and combating ailments removed from him and his only sources of help were an indifferent government and the superstitious practices of the jungle witch doctors.

In the economic world of Jesus the majority of people lived very close to starvation and death. They were constantly being exploited by the rich ruling classes both in the Sanhedrin and in the court of king Herod. A man was not worth the price of a sheep. For the poor people it was fear, suffering; and what little joy they eked out of this world was quickly snuffed out by a hard, merciless, legalistic religion. No wonder Jesus said indignantly to the Pharisees, "Is not a man of more value than a sheep?"

For the poor in the time of Jesus there was little

hope. There was no light or promise of relief.
Their lives consisted of evil tidings, wars, dangers,
superstitions, loneliness, and poverty. It was to
these people that Jesus brought good tidings.
There was a reason why the common people heard
Him gladly. After listening in fear and trembling
to the religious rulers of their time, it was difficult
for the common people to believe that God was as
good and as kind as Jesus. Their problem was
not to believe that Jesus was as good as God but
that God was as good as Jesus. Wherever the Naz-
arene went, the people crowded about Him to
listen to the gracious words which fell from His
lips, or to touch the hem of His garment, or to
call upon Him for mercy for their ailments or for
the sufferings of the members of their families.

The poor had the Gospel preached to them.
They discovered that in the sight of God they
were as valuable as the richly dressed, cultured
Pharisees. The gates of heaven were thrown open
to them, for Jesus said, "Whosoever cometh unto
me, I shall in no wise cast out." He told them the
parables of the lost sheep, the lost coin, and the
prodigal son. Indeed, the last parable should be
spoken of as the parable of the waiting father, for
in this beautiful story Jesus pointed out to His
listeners that whatever their clothes, their station
in life, whatever their physical condition, or their
age; whoever would "come to himself" and humbly kneel before the eternal Father and say,
"Lord, make me as one of thy servants," would
find inner peace upon this earth, and in the hereafter a home eternal not made with hands.

Yes, there was ample evidence to be brought back to John—that the deaf could again hear the voices of their loved ones, that those who had been walking in darkness could see the setting of the sun and catch the expression on the faces of those whom they loved. The lame, stooped and bent, were straightened out and walked as men. And most of all, Jesus brought good tidings to the poor. He preached the Gospel to them and revealed how His power could bring peace and light and hope today and joy hereafter. What a joyous gathering it must have been in that prison when the report was brought back to John of the power and the grace to be found in Jesus Christ!

This incident in the life of John the Baptist should strengthen our faith. John was not the man who could be taken in by sentimental phrases, by a clever flourish of theological knowledge. John was an everyday, down-to-earth man. His acceptance of Jesus as his personal Savior should appeal to the practical man of our day.

In addition we see the unfolding of the Spirit of Christ and how it brought peace and good will upon this earth. Since the death and resurrection of Jesus, His followers have gone up and down the paths of villages, into the markets and streets of our great cities, into our schoolrooms and our homes, and have planted His Word. Slowly and gradually this world has changed.

Jesus said, "I have overcome the world." Wherever the Cross of Christ is lifted up, men are born again. This new creature in Christ immediately sets about to see that the blind receive their sight, the deaf hear, the lame walk, the lepers are healed, and the poor have the Gospel preached to them. Our church historians could give ample evidence of how down through the centuries, like a great wave of light, the Spirit of Christ has rolled over mankind and has brought peace to troubled hearts, health to broken bodies, freedom to those in bondage, hope to those who have been crushed by despair, and comfort to those in sorrow.

We ought not to lay aside this Biblical story by merely rejoicing at the faith of John and the outpouring of the Spirit of God down through the ages. We should also check our own Christian living to see if wherever we live people are drawn to Christ, if justice reigns, if inequality is done away with, if racial hatred is removed, and if men and women seek to help instead of destroy each other.

Long after an atomic bomb is exploded and the immediate effects recorded, there are active, deadly rays which go out from the center of the explosion killing people even days after the sound of the bomb has died out. In an infinitely greater way, and for the good of man, since the historical explosion—the crucifixion of Jesus—there have gone out from it rays not to destroy but to heal and make whole. For the hand of Christ is the hand of life, and whosoever turns to Him will find ample evidence in his own life and in the records of consecrated Christians that Jesus Christ of Nazareth is the eternal Son of God, for He is the same yesterday, today, and forever.

AMEN

Verily I say unto you, Among them that are born of women there hath not arisen a greater than John the Baptist: yet he that is but little in the kingdom of heaven is greater than he. And from the days of John the Baptist until now the kingdom of heaven suffereth violence, and men of violence take it by force. For all the prophets and the law prophesied until John. And if ye are willing to receive it, this is Elijah, that is to come. He that hath ears to hear, let him hear.

MATTHEW 11:11-15

Chapter Eight

Great Men Who Make Us Great

UNLESS the zest for life has entirely abated, all of us long to be greater than we are. And if hope has even a faint glow of the religious we long to be great enough to vindicate our existence here, and some day great enough for God and heaven.

Thomas Carlyle in his essay, "On Heroes and Hero Worship," convincingly develops the thesis that universal history, the history of what man has accomplished in this world, is at bottom the history of the great men who have worked here. He rightfully points out that the very germ of Christianity is a historical person—the greatest of all heroes. History, to Carlyle, is the biography of great men.

The spiritual heritage, development, and destiny of mankind are an integral part of history. Long ago men learned that history is not simply a record of incidents but an analysis of the thinking, aspirations, and philosophies of men. It is historically true that "as a man thinketh in his heart, so is he."

Today's Gospel impresses us with the truth that our spiritual history is also tied up with great men. What we are and can be spiritually is due to the fact that great men have lived before us whose lives still radiate truth and power. Their work and influence are for us either a savor unto life or unto death.

People in Jesus' day were troubled about John the Baptist. Who was he anyway, and what was the significance of his message? Jesus was drawn into the controversy because John had given Him deference and rejoiced when his disciples left to follow Him. It became necessary for Jesus to evaluate for the people John's character and His relation to the wilderness preacher.

John was a great man! So great, Jesus pointed out, that "among them that are born of women there hath not arisen a greater than John the Baptist." But Jesus hastened to add, "Yet he that is but little in the kingdom of heaven is greater than he."

Carlyle calls attention to the fact that men have always seen in nature a revelation of God. "To us also," he says, "through every star, through every blade of grass, is not a God made visible if we will open our mind and eyes?" But Carlyle saw in man, and especially in our incarnate Lord, an infinitely higher revelation of God. He exclaims: "But now of all things whatsoever that we look upon are emblems to us of the Highest God, I add that more so than any of them is man such an emblem."

There are two characters that tower above all others in this season of Advent—John and Jesus. The Advent season is meaningless unless we become acquainted with these men. These men are also so vital in the entire history of the race that even life is an insolvable riddle unless we understand their person and mission and take the right relation to both of them.

John and Jesus are so significant that for us they become emblems of eternal truth. John is the emblem of the Law and Jesus is the emblem of the Gospel. In the latter case, He is more than an emblem—He is the Gospel!

It is necessary to have a meeting with John the Baptist if we are to possess Christian faith and have a genuine Christian experience. Advent is a season of preparation. The Christ of Christmas is coming and we are to prepare to meet Him. John was the man whom God sent to prepare the way for Jesus. Isaiah foresaw the forerunner seven hundred years before and prophesied, "The voice of one that crieth, Prepare ye in the wilderness the way of the Lord: make level in the desert a highway for our God. Every valley shall be exalted, and every mountain and hill shall be made low; and the uneven shall be made level, and the rough places a plain, and the glory of the Lord shall be revealed, and all flesh shall see it together; for the mouth of the Lord hath spoken it" (Isaiah 40:3-5).

In ancient times, before established roads and communications, when a king was to visit his domain it was necessary for a messenger to go several days before him so that his subjects could prepare a road for him and his train and plan his reception. Christ is a king, but His kingdom is within the hearts of men. So the wilderness of which the prophet spoke—with its valleys, mountains, hills, uneven and rough places—was within the hearts of men. And the highway of God was to be within the hearts of men, even though they were nothing but a wilderness of sin, ignorance, and unbelief.

As the roadbuilder for the Son of God, John's only equipment was a voice. It was the Voice of the Law. Men had to come to a knowledge of sin and long for deliverance before they would be ready to receive a Savior. So John thundered at the people in the language of Sinai, "Ye offspring of vipers, who warned you to flee from the wrath to come? Bring forth therefore fruit worthy of repentance; and think not within yourselves, We have Abraham to our father: for I say unto you, that God is able of these stones to raise up children unto Abraham. And even now the axe lieth at the root of the trees: every tree therefore that bringeth not forth good fruit is hewn down and cast into the fire. I indeed baptize you in water unto repentance, but he that cometh after me is mightier than I, whose shoes I am not worthy to bear: he shall baptize you in the Holy Spirit and in fire: whose fan is in his hand, and he will thoroughly cleanse his threshing floor; and he will gather his wheat into the garner, but the chaff he will burn up with unquenchable fire" (Matthew 3:7-12) .

Such preaching convicted of sin and struck terror in people's hearts so they asked, "What then must we do?" (Luke 3:10).

Unless we meet John and listen to his message, we shall sleep in our sins and believe that we are sufficiently good in ourselves. In our spiritual blindness the Law as stated in the Ten Commandments and the Golden Rule will become a "way of salvation," for we shall little realize how far short we fall in keeping it. But in John, the Law, we meet the reality of sin and see ourselves as sinners. John, as the emblem of the Law, must become our schoolmaster to lead us to Christ.

Our generation has heard much about a new approach to the scriptures. Thank God for scientific textual criticism that makes for and assures purity of text. While we believe the autographs of the scriptures were inspired, we do not consider the manuscripts and translations in our possession today infallible. Errors have been made and additions crept in as the scriptures have been handed down from generation to generation. But all so-called textual criticism has not been scientific. Much of it has been wild speculation, built on absurd hypotheses. Yet so far as the cardinal doctrines of scripture are concerned, the late Dr. Reu pointed out that the most radical conclusions of the critics with respect to the Bible text itself would not erase or alter one article of the historic Christian faith.

How many the books about the Bible: *A Guide to Understanding the Bible, The Modern Use of the Scriptures, The Bible and the Common*

Reader. We have no fears as to what sound scholarship may do with the text of the scriptures, nor with the interpretation that true historical and archeological research will give. Such investigation we sincerely welcome.

Yet the key that opens the scriptures is not the tools and methods of modern scholarship, but the right understanding of Law and Gospel in the unfolding of God's revelation to man in the words of the Bible. Until we see the difference between Law and Gospel the Bible is a closed book and we have no legal or moral right to call ourselves Christians. The context of the Bible contains two teachings: Law and Gospel. The Law part of the Bible tells us what we should do, and then it makes clear to us that Law is not a way of salvation as man lacks that love which is the fulfilling of the Law. The Gospel part tells us of God's grace in Jesus Christ. But we are not ready for the Gospel until the Law has brought us under the reality of sin, imperfection, and condemnation. We have to feel John's axe before we are willing to accept Jesus' forgiving grace.

That which is the historical order of Advent is also the order in our heart's experience of true Christianity. As John came before Jesus, so Law must be preached before Gospel; sin must become a reality before grace can be appropriated; repentance must precede faith.

Often spiritually awakened people wonder why there is so little conviction of sin today, so few seeking the Lord, so many indifferent toward God's commands and the work of His kingdom, so cold the passion for souls, so hazy the hope concerning an everlasting life. The answer is that the majority have failed to have a real session with John the Baptist, the great man of the Law.

John kept on preaching Law until there was genuine hunger and thirst for righteousness in the lives of his hearers. Then one day as John was preaching on the banks of the Jordan, a lone figure came over the horizon. Now John was to decrease and the Man in the distance was to increase. The thunderings of the Law were to give way to the glad tidings of the Gospel. John changed his text and pointing to the One who was infinitely greater than himself exclaimed, "Behold the Lamb of God that taketh away the sin of the world" (John 1:29). The Gospel falls on deaf ears unless the Law has first unstopped them.

Jesus said that "from the days of John the Baptist until now the kingdom of heaven suffereth violence, and men of violence take it by force." This does not refer to the persecution of the kingdom by its enemies, nor to the advancement of the kingdom by violent means (for this statement explains the greatness of John), but to the violent bursting forth of the kingdom of heaven out of the kernel of the Old Testament law, ordinances, and prophets. John and Jesus are the violent who take it by force. The former begins the assault and the latter completes the conquest. It is a figurative description of the power, zeal, and persistency that characterize the emerging and progress of the kingdom of heaven.

Moffatt puts it into modern English: "From the days of John the Baptist until now, they are pressing into the realm of heaven—these eager souls are storming it."

No one storms the realm of heaven until he has met John the Baptist. Apart from a knowledge and experience of law, sin, and repentance there will never be a religion of love, life, and power which men will propagate with zeal and enthusiasm, and, if need be, die for.

It is proper that in the church all things be done decently and in order and that God be worshipped in the beauty of holiness. But sometimes this is reduced to just "pretty stuff" that leaves no room for John the Baptist. Religion becomes merely an esthetic experience that conveys nothing more than sugary sentiment and leaves the mind and heart virtually untouched so far as the real issues of life are concerned. Too often there is in reality no difference between so-called Christian worship and the viewing of a first-rate technicolor film.

Call in John the Baptist, the great man with the Law! The Christian Church cannot be Christ's church without the message of the Law preached as rugged and unadorned as a John clothed with camel's hair and a leathern girdle and with a diet of locusts and wild honey. The preacher who does not know John the Baptist is in Jesus' sight an effeminate sycophant with spiritual armament no better than soft raiment and with no more moral stamina than a reed shaken with the wind.

John the Baptist shows us what we need to be

saved from, who can save us, and what we are saved to do. As the emblem of the Law he "convicts us of sin and God's wrath against sin; he alarms us and drives us to seek Christ; he shows believers the fruits that faith should bear."

Only when we have met the great man, John, are we ready to meet the greater man, Jesus. In fact, the greater Jesus will not meet anyone that has not been taught law, sin, and repentance by the great John. The truth of the matter is that no one who has not had a meeting with John the Baptist cares a whit about Jesus. This accounts for the negative attitude toward Jesus on the part of most people in the world today. Jesus cannot make them well because John has never been permitted to show them they are sick. "They that be whole have no need of a physician, but they that are sick" (Matthew 9:12).

Jesus is the Gospel, the Great Physician, who heals and restores after John, the Law, has exposed our terrible sickness and revealed our needs. Law never heals and regenerates. Law only coerces and makes transgressions alive. Some power must cleanse the inner man and transform character so that the whole man is made harmonious to the will of God. Only Jesus, who is the Gospel, can do this. For while Jesus is Man, He is *the* Man, because He is God Himself who did for us what the Law could not, by coming Himself in the likeness of sinful flesh to condemn sin in the flesh: "that the ordinance of the Law might be fulfilled in us, who walk not after the flesh, but after the Spirit" (Romans 8:1-4).

Although John of the Law was a great man, Jesus of the Gospel makes all who believe in Him greater than John. "Among them that are born of women there hath not arisen a greater than John the Baptist: yet he that is but little in the kingdom of heaven is greater than he."

John was the connecting link between the Old and New Covenants, between shadow and reality. He belonged entirely neither to the Old nor the New. He was an Elijah that foretold the Lord's coming, but he was also the herald who announced that He had come.

No one in Old Testament times had seen what John saw of the truth and ways of God. He was greater not as a prophet or in righteousness and sincerity, but in spiritual privilege, knowledge and experience.

Yet Jesus declares that even the least in the kingdom of heaven is greater than John. Our spiritual knowledge, riches, privileges, and experiences are infinitely greater and larger than those of John. Although John saw and talked with Him, the work of redemption had not been sealed by Jesus' death and resurrection, and the Holy Spirit had not come to dwell among believers in His official capacity as the revealer of Jesus because Jesus was not yet glorified. The least in the kingdom of heaven today can view the finished work of redemption and possess the witness and power and comfort of the Holy Spirit.

No wonder Jesus says to us, "He that hath ears to hear, let him hear." We stand in the inheritance of those to whom Jesus said, "Many prophets

and righteous men desired to see the things which
ye see, and saw them not, and to hear the things
which ye hear, and heard them not" (Matthew
13:17).

Jesus is the Gospel! It is the gift and power of
the Gospel that makes even the most insignificant
Christian greater than John the Baptist. In fact,
Jesus makes us just as great in God's sight as He
is. That is the glory and truth of the incarnation!
Jesus' life becomes our life; His righteousness, our
righteousness; His death, our death; His grace,
our grace; His resurrection, our resurrection; His
heaven, our heaven; His Father, our Father.

Yes, any truly great man influences and molds
the generations that come after him. But today we
have met the Greatest Man of all history and a
great man through whom we can come to know
Him. If we but follow the truth of John, the Law,
and Jesus, the Gospel, we can become as great in
God's sight as Jesus is great!

AMEN

Now in the fifteenth year of the reign of Tiberius Cæsar, Pontius Pilate being governor of Judæa, and Herod being tetrarch of Galilee, and his brother Philip tetrarch of the region of Ituræa and Trachonitis, and Lysanias tetrarch of Abilene, in the high-priesthood of Annas and Caiaphas, the word of God came unto John the son of Zacharias in the wilderness. And he came into all the region round about the Jordan, preaching the baptism of repentance unto remission of sins; as it is written in the book of the words of Isaiah the prophet, The voice of one crying in the wilderness, Make ye ready the way of the Lord, make his paths straight. Every valley shall be filled, and every mountain and hill shall be brought low; and the crooked shall become straight, and the rough ways smooth; and all flesh shall see the salvation of God.

LUKE 3:1-6

Chapter Nine

Practical Repentance

THE well-known story of the preaching of John the Baptist lies before us.

We think of John as the man who was sent to prepare the way for the coming of Jesus. He was the king's herald; "the voice," as Isaiah the prophet had said, "of one crying in the wilderness, Make ye ready the way of the Lord." He was a mighty preacher, and a true prophet of God, who preached for results, and got them. What those results were, and what the preaching was that brought them about, we shall consider as we study the theme, "Practical Repentance."

We do not mean to imply that true repentance is ever impractical. It depends, of course, upon the goal at which you aim. If you seek peace of conscience, or if your need is the remission of sins, repentance, as we shall see, is practical because it is the only way that works. It might be otherwise if you seek other goals. However, we use the term "practical" now in another sense, as the opposite of a "theoretical" repentance. We could just as well have said "real repentance"; for what we mean is a repentance that is genuine, that is living and active; in other words, the real thing.

It was such a repentance that John preached, and it brought results.

The keynote to his ministry, as it must be the keynote to the ministry of any man who earnestly seeks to prepare the way for Jesus Christ into human hearts, is expressed in the one powerful, significant word, "Repent!" "Repent ye; for the kingdom of heaven is at hand," were the words that summed up his preaching. The historian says of him that "he came—preaching the baptism of repentance unto remission of sins." That was preaching to the crowds; but the theme was the same when he preached to the individual, no matter who it might be. Who does not remember his courageous rebuke of Herod's sin in taking his brother's wife! John paid for that sermon with his life; but who shall say that it was in vain? The influence of a powerful preacher of repentance often continues long after he is dead. That was true of the great Hebrew prophets who preceded John, and in whose footsteps he followed. They were one and all mighty preachers of repentance even when not using the term itself; and the repercussions of their preaching can be felt still. The modern world simply cannot escape the heart-searching of the moral, spiritual, and social message of the prophets, wherein sins were labeled as sins, and the need of the saving intervention of

God in human affairs was set forth in a way that cannot be denied.

To this succession of the prophets John belonged. True, as Jesus testified, he was "much more than a prophet." That was because of the uniqueness of his position as the messenger who should come immediately before the Messiah and prepare the way for Him in that very generation. The prophets had predicted his coming as the final prophetic voice crying in the wilderness of human need to make ready the way for the coming of the Savior. Luke, the sacred historian, identifies John's Jordan ministry with the fulfillment of this prediction. So significant does he regard it, not for its own sake only, but because of the nearness of the Christ for whom it prepared the way, that he takes pains to date it in the most exact manner possible. Roman emperor and Jewish high-priest, and local governors in all the regions most concerned, are named, in order to mark the exact moment when "the word of God came unto John the son of Zacharias in the wilderness, and he came into all the region round about the Jordan; preaching the baptism of repentance."

But the historian does not stop when he has said that John preached repentance. A true repentance is the preparation for the coming of Jesus. It opens the ear to hear and the heart to receive the Gospel of Christ, with its promise of the forgiveness of sins. John preached repentance, but not as an end in itself; he preached it as a means unto the remission of sins. We must not, because we may not, separate these two. Repentance is never more than a preparation; the real goal is remission of sins, the salvation of God. If in our preaching we preach repentance only we stop short of the goal of God; we do not attain unto faith and hope and love. But on the other hand, if there is to be forgiveness, there must be sincere repentance. God cannot forgive him who finds pleasure in his sin, to whom the world is still too precious to let go. There are glorious promises of pardon in the Word of God, promises for sinners who repent; but they are spoken to the repentant only. We need the preaching of John; for if we want to be forgiven and to find peace with God we must first repent. There is no other way. We must turn our back upon sin. We must desire to quit it. We must turn our face toward God. We must pray that His good, and holy, and perfect will be done toward us, and also by us. We must repent if we are to be saved. That is the inescapable conclusion from the historical ministry of John as a preparation for the ministry of Jesus. Spiritually it works that way still.

For what does it mean to repent? There is something robust and compelling about the very sound of the word; yet we need to make sure that it has in our hearts and minds the clear ring of a command that is understood. That is the more true of practical repentance; for we cannot act if we do not know what God would have us do, and we will not act unless we see the compelling urgency of each step that the Spirit of God who works repentance would have us take.

Practical repentance is first of all *a conviction*

of sin. Perhaps we need to say that again, and in a different way: it is the conviction born within me that *I* have sinned. There can be no real repentance until conscience has begun to speak. We must know that we have sinned, and that our sin is no trifling, laughing matter; that because of it we have come short of the glory of God. It need not always be a conviction of some special sin that we have committed, although that is where it usually begins. Sometimes, however, it is an overwhelming sense of sinfulness and shortcoming which we cannot quite analyze. Yet the painful awareness of sin in myself, and the realization that my sins condemn me before God, is the only root out of which a genuine repentance can grow.

If you have never felt this conviction of sin in your heart you have certainly never repented, no matter how confidently you can talk about the sins of others. Practical repentance begins with a personal experience of the conviction of sin. The first sign of its presence is a wide-awake, alert, sensitive, accusing conscience; a conscience that has come in headlong collision with the stubborn fact of sin as seen in my own life in the light of the Word of God which so relentlessly exposes sin against both God and man.

Practical repentance is also *a change of heart* with regard to sin. How important to remember this truth when we seek repentance in ourselves and others! There can be no real repentance until we in our hearts turn away from sin; until we cease to love it, and to cling to it, and to cherish it, and to defend it; until we begin instead to hate it, and to loathe it, and to desire to put it away; until we say with the Psalmist, "I will be sorry for my sin." There is a sense in which repentance means to make a clean break with sin; for when we repent we turn our backs upon sin, and our faces toward God.

Mark well that this change of heart does not rid us of our sin. It takes more than repentance on my part to do that. A change of heart is not to be confused with a clean heart. It is only the forgiveness of God that can make the heart clean; but before there can be the experience of forgiveness there must come the experience of a changed heart with respect to the sin that makes it unclean. We may call it also a changed attitude. We might even call it a change of direction. Paul, you remember, was sent to preach to the Gentiles "that they may turn from darkness to light and from the power of Satan unto God" (Acts 26:18). Practical repentance means just such a turning from sin unto God; and this turning takes place first in our hearts, when our whole attitude toward all things sinful, whether in ourselves or in others, undergoes a change.

"I will be sorry for my sin," said the Psalmist. How better express the change of heart of which we have been speaking! The old word for it (and it was a good word) was contrition. I am not sure that most people today know what that means. It means far more than a casual regret over some slight misdeed. It is an emotion that hurts! And yet, unlike remorse, which also hurts, the sorrow of contrition is a godly sorrow that does not brood

over the past, but turns in trembling hope to the
God of grace against whom we have sinned. The
sorrow is none the less deep because there is hope
joined with it. The contrite sinner grieves over
his sin because the sin grieves God. That is an
even deeper sorrow than the sorrow because of
the evil consequences of sin to ourselves; yet who
can be happy over being a failure or when the
voice of conscience and the law of God condemn?
Then, too, there is the added sorrow because of
the grief that we so often cause unto others when
we sin. Our sin has this threefold aspect: it affects
God, ourselves, and others. The contrition which
is the very heart of true repentance must do the
same. Only so does it become a true change of
heart; only so does it permit God to give us a clean
heart. Without contrition for sin there is no
promise of cleansing; there is no room for the
Savior, no room for Jesus, who because of sin,
yours and mine, had to die the death of the Cross.
Should not that move us to tears?

But practical repentance has not only a heart.
It has a voice, and that voice is *a true confession*
before God that "I have sinned."

The prodigal son comes to mind as an example.
When he had experienced a change of heart, or
"when he came to himself," as the Scripture says,
he resolved to say, "Father, I have sinned against
heaven, and in thy sight: I am no more worthy to
be called thy son: make me as one of thy hired
servants" (Luke 15:18-19)

I have sinned! Those are hard words to say; yet
practical repentance, true repentance, must bring

you and me to the place of confession where we too must speak words such as these. We have sinned. Have we also confessed the sin? We are unworthy. Have we also confessed our unworthiness? Have we really admitted in our hearts before God, and with our lips unto God, that we are worthy to be cast away from His presence if He should judge us according to our sins? Have we besought Him to be forgiven as if we really needed to be forgiven? If we have never done that, we have never repented. If we don't know the shame and the sorrow with which a genuine confession of sin is squeezed out of the human heart and forced over human lips, we do not know anything about practical repentance. For practical repentance must end in a plea for mercy. It cannot keep quiet. It compels to prayer. No need of coaxing the repentant sinner to pray! He cannot keep from praying. He must pray or perish! There is no peace for him until he asks for pardon; and even then the peace does not come by the prayer. It does not come until he knows in his heart on the authority of God's own Word that he can be pardoned, yes, that he is pardoned when he looks to Jesus for salvation.

When Paul was convicted of the sin of persecuting Christ and the Church, he began to pray. Of that prayer we have no copy. Did he turn, as so many others have turned, to the Contrite Sinner's Prayer for Pardon in the Old Testament prayer-book? For when David was convicted of his sin against Uriah and Bathsheba he began to pray; and this prayer is recorded in the 51st Psalm. Only

God knows how often this psalm has served as the prayer of other penitent sinners like David. But whether in words borrowed or in words all his own, whenever any sinner truly repents he also prays; for repentance without prayer is a contradiction. Repentance ends in prayer!

Ends in prayer, did we say? No, that would not be strictly true. Rather say that it ends in *the remission of sins*. It prepares the way for the Savior to come into our hearts with all the fulness of His grace and blessing; speaking peace to the broken-hearted; meeting the confession "I have sinned" with the assurance, "Thy sin is forgiven," and answering the plea, "Have mercy upon me," with the promise, "I will! Go in peace."

John's ministry, historically, was to preach repentance, and thereby to level off mountains and to fill up valleys and to prepare a straight, smooth, level way for the Lord Jesus, in whom men should see the salvation of God. It would have been tragedy to stop with the ministry of John. It would be tragedy still if we stopped with repentance and spoke no word of that which is the sinner's need, the remission of sins. Thanks be to God—when we repent, God forgives! The last word does not belong to the sinner but to the Savior. It is not the sentence of a publican's penitent prayer but the promise of a gracious God who justifies sinners through faith in Jesus Christ.

> True belief, and true repentance,
> Every grace that brings us nigh,
> Without money,
> Come to Jesus Christ, and buy.

Let not conscience make you linger,
  Nor of fitness fondly dream;
All the fitness He requireth,
  Is to feel your need of Him;
  This He gives you;
  'Tis His Spirit's rising beam.

JOSEPH HART

This is to behold the glory of God! And yet, strange as it may seem, practical repentance does not end even here, in the experience of peace in the forgiveness of sins. For practical repentance is something more than words. It touches the whole life. It begins in the heart. It puts words of prayer upon the lips. It leads up to the experience of forgiveness. But it also brings forth *fruits worthy of repentance*. It has a life as well as a voice through which it expresses itself.

Such was the preaching of John the Baptist. He preached the baptism of repentance unto remission of sins; but he did not stop there. He preached also the need of proving your repentance with your life. The change of heart must carry over into a newness of life. For what is the ultimate purpose of repentance? Is it this that our hearts might be prepared to call upon Jesus, our Savior, to have mercy upon us and to forgive us all our sins? No, it is not! That is *not* the ultimate or final purpose of repentance (or of redemption). Repentance is not complete until it compels us to seek a new manner of life; until we begin to ask, because we really want to know, "What must we do, not only to be saved, but as those that have been saved through faith in Jesus Christ?"

John's preaching brought results. The folks who heard him became deeply concerned to know what to do; and John told them! To the multitudes he said, "He that hath two coats, let him impart to him that hath none; and he that hath food, let him do likewise." That is to say, repentance means that we turn away from a life of selfishness to a life of love. To the publicans, whose peculiar sin was that of squeezing out more money in taxes than they were entitled to, he said, "Extort no more than that which is appointed you." Or as Weymouth so excellently translates, "Do not exact more than the legal amount." To the soldiers he said, "Extort from no man by violence, neither accuse any one wrongfully; and be content with your wages." In each case the fruits of repentance correspond to the besetting sin of the individual.

It should be so also with us. If the sin be drunkenness, the fruits worthy of repentance are temperance, self-control, and a loving care as well as a good example for others. You have not repented of the sin until you earnestly seek these fruits. That is involved in the very change of heart that precedes forgiveness. Your repentance is not complete or at an end until these fruits may be seen in your life. If the sin be selfishness, the fruits worthy of repentance are love and thoughtfulness for others, and the willingness to sacrifice comfort and ease in serving them. If the sin be greed, or the love of money, repentance should not make a careless spendthrift out of you, but it should bring forth the fruits of generosity and of helpfulness in all human need. If the sin be unkindness in act or judgment, the fruits worthy of repentance are charity, and humility, and the kindly word, and the kindlier deed.

We cannot run the whole gamut of sins and point out all the fruits worthy of repentance. That would take too long! It would be a glorious experience, however, if we would prepare room for Christ in our lives as well as in our hearts, by asking earnestly, in the spirit of true repentance, "What then must we do?" What are the fruits of repentance, the fruits of the Spirit, if you will, that God wants to see among us, in you, in me? If we ask the question because we really want to know and to obey, God will supply the answer. He will tell you what to do. Do you dare to ask? Do you care to know? Will you let the Holy Spirit show you what practical repentance means for you—a conviction of sin—a change of heart—a true confession of sin in sincere and earnest prayer— a life that shows a constant and sincere desire to bring forth fruits worthy of repentance?

The power must come from God, through His Word and by His Spirit; but He will supply the power if we are willing to receive. Repent, unto remission of sins, and bear fruit worthy of the Spirit who works true repentance! So shall all flesh see the salvation of God, as Christ becomes Savior and Lord in repentant human hearts and lives.

AMEN

And this is the witness of John, when the Jews sent unto him from Jerusalem priests and Levites to ask him, Who art thou? And he confessed, and denied not; and he confessed, I am not the Christ. And they asked him, What then? Art thou Elijah? And he saith, I am not. Art thou the prophet? And he answered, No. They said therefore unto him, Who art thou? that we may give an answer to them that sent us. What sayest thou of thyself? He said, I am the voice of one crying in the wilderness, Make straight the way of the Lord, as said Isaiah the prophet. And they had been sent from the Pharisees. And they asked him, and said unto him, Why then baptizest thou, if thou art not the Christ, neither Elijah, neither the prophet? John answered them, saying, I baptize with water: in the midst of you standeth one whom ye know not, even he that cometh after me, the latchet of whose shoe I am not worthy to unloose. These things were done in Bethany beyond the Jordan, where John was baptizing.

JOHN 1:19-28

Chapter Ten

The Voice of One Crying

DURING many millenniums uncounted voices had been crying in the wilderness of sin, searching for a Deliverer. He was sought for on thrones, in palaces, and among warriors. Empires rose and fell. Conquerors came and made the world more miserable. The weary centuries waited. No one expected to find Him in a barn among the lowly cattle.

In those stirring Advent days, Herod was troubled, and all Jerusalem with him. John the Baptist was the morning star, heralding the advent of the great Deliverer. When the dawn comes, the morning star decreases, the sun dispels the darkness, and the world stirs after the night.

It is no wonder that all Jerusalem and Judea were aroused and went down to the Jordan to hear the greatest preacher ever born to woman before the time of Christ. The great Supreme Court of the Jews, the Sanhedrin, sent an embassy to inquire about the cause of the stir. It was perfectly proper that the Sanhedrin should look into the matter. That august body represented the Church of God in that day. Church leaders in synods and congregations should be inquisitive about the preachers and the doctrines they preach. The Church has no right to be careless about its teachers. They inquired, "Who art thou?"

Let us meditate upon the answer John sent back to the Levites, Scribes, and Pharisees of his day. Let us finally decide what our verdict is to be regarding the voice of one crying in the wilderness.

What Did That Voice Cry About Himself and His Work?

John had no illusions about himself. That noble figure bore unfaltering witness to the Messiah and directed his loved disciples to Jesus. "His uprightness, candor, humility, boldness, and power form traits of a character that wins the esteem and admiration of all noble minds. But now his work is nearly done—and well done. Therefore, like a modest herald he steps aside at the coming of the Prince whose way he had prepared."

Pious Israelites, and some even among the formalists, wondered if John the Baptist might be the Messiah. "The people were in expectation" (Luke 3:15). They asked John, "Who art thou?"

John made no delay in giving his answer. "He confessed, and denied not." He had no thought as to his own honor or self-advantage. With striking brevity he declared that he was neither Christ, nor the Prophet, nor Elijah. He would not exalt himself. He was a *voice!* His office, not he himself, was important. He drew attention away from himself to the Messiah. He himself was the *voice of one crying* (Isaiah 40:3) . "A man becomes a voice when he desires nothing for himself, when he does not consider himself, but when his message is everything" (Luther)

John looked at his people and saw a wilderness of sin, a people who needed to be "prepared for the Lord" (Luke 1:16-18, 76) by true repentance.

John's voice was so powerful that a little bit of flirting with the Sanhedrin would have crowned him king. He might have been worshiped. But John did not give Satan one moment's time to ruin him with pride. Satan was once an angel, then became a serpent instead of a servant at the throne. Some men are weak; they yield to a treacherous nature; they stop to wait on Satan, then fall in ruinous pride. John was quick to confess that he was not the Christ, nor the Prophet, nor even Elijah. He declared himself to be a voice crying in the wilderness.

It is not strange that the Sanhedrin wondered if John might be Elijah. Both were men of the wilderness; both were plain men; both were orators; Elijah at Carmel was as great as John at the Jordan. Elijah left for heaven in a fiery chariot from the very place where John was preaching that day.

John plainly declared who he was not. He took no false honors to himself. But he also made plain who he was. He was not hesitant about that.

He regarded himself as a poor humble preacher. He was neither pope nor sacerdotal priest. He was no divine mediator between God and man. He did not claim divine honors for his person. He was only a voice crying. He would not stand between the seeking sinner and the seeking Savior. He made no pretense by strutting in great parade. Appearances made little difference to him. He would hide himself in order to reveal his Lord. He wanted his hearers to know that he had a voice, a God-given voice, a voice which he raised in a great cry to the people in order to warn of sin and to herald the Savior. He cared nothing for fame. So far from being the Christ, he felt unworthy to stand on a level with the shoestrings of his Lord's sandals. "The true height of man in this world is the lowest humility."

But while John declared himself to be a voice, a humble preacher, he was a faithful preacher. He gave his all to his ministry. He was a voice crying! His earnestness was intense. He saw that the world was in perishing need of the Christ. He was bound to let every ear that would hear listen to his voice.

Every man must hear the Gospel story of salvation or be lost—that was plain to John who had entered the kingdom on his knees. John gave everything to his ministry. He sought to please no man, but God only.

God wants His ministers to make the way straight. John warned the Pharisees, he warned the Scribes, he warned all to repent of sin lest they be damned and perish. Such a ministry is needed today. It is time that every minister cuts a straight path for his people. No man can be counted better than his business, his pleasures, or his habits. In every pulpit today we need John the Baptists who will fear neither man nor devil.

John the Baptist was a preacher who did not apologize for the God-given *means of grace*. He baptized with water. He delivered the message entrusted to him by his Master. He was no great one who could do better than the divine command. He was sent of God to be a witness of the Light. He had no message of his own to deliver. He accepted the Old Testament as the Word of God. He proclaimed the revealed Word. He knew the story about the Paschal Lamb. He pointed to Jesus as the Lamb of God who bore the sin of the world. He baptized Jesus Christ by the authority of God. He was true to his commission. Even today God comes to His people through the sacraments of Baptism and the Lord's Supper.

John further witnesses that Jesus was before him even though born six months after him. He witnesses to the eternity of Jesus. He regards himself as a poor, insignificant messenger of God while his voice cries in the wilderness witnessing to the incarnation of God in Jesus Christ.

What Did That Voice Cry About Christ and His Work?

John did not at first recognize the destiny of Jesus. John's humble cousin at Nazareth did not look like the Messiah. It was at His baptism that John saw the Redeemer. Mary's son was there re-

vealed as the Son of God. Somehow it did not
seem right that one so pure should have the baptism of remission of sin. "John's baptism, like the
Old Testament offerings, was intimately related
to the forgiveness of sin. And as the offerer was
purged from sin by looking in faith toward what
those offerings symbolized, so those who received
John's baptism in faith as a preparation for the
coming of God's kingdom, participated in that
forgiveness which membership in that kingdom
implies. But, like the Old Testament offerings,
this baptism was typical and temporary. It could
not confer that spiritual life by which renewed
men are enabled 'to mortify the deeds of the body'
(Romans 8:13)." It was revealed to John at
Christ's baptism that it was He who "should baptize with the Holy Ghost." So John was ready to
testify that in baptism Christ had become High
Priest, Prophet, and King. The fullness of the
God-head dwelt in Him bodily. God was manifest
in the flesh.

John exalted Christ. He did not regard Christ
as an ungrateful and presumptuous usurper.
Though John was eclipsed by Jesus, he still received more than he gave. It is a comfort to true
preachers to see others follow them with greater
success. True greatness is never sullen. As John's
crowds grew smaller, and his time shorter, he was
the more industrious. He consigned his interests
to his greater Successor. He was content to go out
of date, for his mission was fulfilled. He rejoiced
in Christ's humiliation which made Him to dwell
in the flesh as the Bridegroom. It is true He chose

a humble bride, but the choice was His. John rejoiced to hear the voice of Jesus and then cried as a voice in the wilderness proclaiming the Bridegroom's advent. He rejoiced in Christ's person, a Being before conception and birth. He rejoiced in the excellency and certainty of Christ's doctrines. They were infallible, sure, and certain. John rejoiced in Christ's power and authority. Angels were His servants and devils were His captives. He was the Father's Plenipotentiary, Lawgiver, Almoner, and Judge. Christ was not a vessel, but the Fountain. Indeed, John saw in Christ a great Savior, One able to save to the uttermost, One competent to bear the guilt of all sin, One qualified to break the prison of the soul asunder, One powerful enough to destroy the works of the devil, One fitted to burst sin's every fetter.

And yet, John saw in Christ one not too great. He was no modernist minimizing Christ's divinity. He could not do without a single claim made by Jesus. His Savior must needs be great and sublime in order to save from sin and the power of the devil. Whoever has gained some insight into the atrociousness, the unexampled power, the infinite guilt of his own sins, will understand and realize that in order to be saved he needs a Savior no less than that One depicted in Holy Writ.

John heralded an indispensable Savior coming. Christ is the link which connects God and humanity. "He that believes on the Son hath eternal life." He who believeth not must bid farewell to the hope of eternal life and salvation.

This sort of faith and testimony is not made cheaply. John passed through all the degrees of doubt which beset any of us today. John had given his name, reputation, popularity, and at last his life for Christ. Let the centuries answer the question, "Did it pay?"

But, alas, John cried despairingly, because no man received his testimony. Hardly any believed his testimony, but still he cried as one in the wilderness.

What Shall Be Our Cry in the Winderness of To-day?

Let us first remember to be grateful for faithful and steadfast preachers. As John confessed Christ, so he was confessed by Christ (cf. Matt. 11:2-10). It is better to follow good leaders than to be without them. Those worth hearing are worth recollecting. Thank God for spiritual leaders who are firm, resolute, and unwavering amid popular applause or in the fierce and blustering storms of criticism. Thank God for self-denying men who are mortified to this world's temptations. Let us be grateful for men of God who preach the doctrines of sin and grace, of penitence and repentance. Jesus preferred John to all others. Jesus still prefers preachers who proclaim the doctrine of remission to penitent and believing souls. To such the heavens open and upon them the Holy Dove descends.

God owned John's ministry and made it successful. He was rejected by the Scribes, Pharisees, Levites, and Priests, but his ministry was owned by Christ. Jesus rejoiced to see the results of one crying in the wilderness because the way of the Lord was made straight. The violent took the kingdom by force. The kingdom of heaven was never intended for the indulgence of triflers.

John's cry must precede Christ's, as the Law must precede the Gospel. There was a revival in John's day, people asked how they might gain entrance into the kingdom of God. John preached the kingdom *at hand;* we preach the kingdom *is here!* Forgiveness, rest, peace are yours—if you repent, renounce sin, and believe in Jesus.

As we approach the birthday of Jesus Christ, let us cry out to the world that He is the King of Kings. Jesus is the final Savior of the race; He is the final and absolute revelation of God; He sweeps away all previous teachings contrary to His Word; He claims personal loyalty and vigorous obedience from all of His subjects; He claims and proves His holiness; and He is the final Judge of all men. All of this is proved within the Gospels, in the course of history, in the fulfillments of prophecy, and in the personal devotion of His countless followers.

The cry of the world is a denial of the cry of John and his followers. The cries of faithless Priests and Levites are subtle criticisms emanating from unbelieving scholarship. The results of unrepentance are found in Esau seeking with tears, in Saul whose spirit departed, in Jeroboam who finds himself cut off from the sanctuary of God, or in Judas who finds himself gone out into darkness forever.

In the midst of us standeth one whom many know not. Let our voices cry in the wilderness of today. Jesus is the King. His kingdom is not a temporal one; it is a spiritual kingdom. His palace is in the hearts of the believers; His throne is on the cross; and His crown was one made of thorns. Let this way of salvation be made straight.

The people known as His followers were not princes in waiting or gentlemen-at-arms. They were humble fishermen whose nobility was service. Christ's glory was their chief aim and His law was the delight of their souls. Wealth is no part of their glory and they usually ride in the poorest state. Their riches are not gold, but faith. His is a kingdom without armed force, and victory comes through *His* efforts and grace alone. It is a kingdom of peace. His Church is not founded upon the doctrine of force. His dogmas are not proclaimed by war drums. His armies are loving thoughts; His troops are kind words and benedictions. His kingdom is quite lacking in worldly pomp. Strangely lacking are dresses, costumes, trumpets, tapestried streets, fountains of wine, and worldly excitement. He has founded a kingdom of meekness, faith, and love. He is on a colt today, on the cross tomorrow, and the Judge of the earth very soon.

Yes, and we should cry to the world that here is a kingdom without taxations, and where values are ever steadfast. Citizens are found everywhere. They feel their gifts are too little, so they give themselves away. It is a kingdom of true joy. The ordinary king sheds the blood of his subjects, opens fountains of tears, and creates uncounted widows and orphans. His trumpets seek to cover up the cries, sorrows, and agonies. But in the triumphs of King Jesus, the repentant sinner finds all tears wiped away while he is lifted up to the throne.

Let every redeemed soul join in the wilderness cry. Let the cry be as intense as was that of John. Let the despairing soul arise and cry, "Hosanna," for Christianity is not dull, lifeless, and insipid. Let the blind see, the halt run, the deaf hear, and the dead awake. Let all join in the cry; let all make the way of the Lord straight.

The most blessed of earth are the subjects of the divine King. Blessed is He who comes in the name of the Lord.

AMEN

After these things came Jesus and his disciples into the land of Judæa; and there he tarried with them, and baptized. And John also was baptizing in Ænon near to Salim, because there was much water there: and they came, and were baptized. For John was not yet cast into prison. There arose therefore a questioning on the part of John's disciples with a Jew about purifying. And they came unto John, and said unto him, Rabbi, he that was with thee beyond the Jordan, to whom thou hast borne witness, behold, the same baptizeth, and all men come to him. John answered and said, A man can receive nothing, except it have been given him from heaven. Ye yourselves bear me witness, that I said, I am not the Christ, but, that I am sent before him. He that hath the bride is the bridegroom: but the friend of the bridegroom, that standeth and heareth him, rejoiceth greatly because of the bridegroom's voice: this my joy is therefore made full. He must increase, but I must decrease. He that cometh from above is above all: he that is of the earth is of the earth, and of the earth he speaketh: he that cometh from heaven is above all. What he hath seen and heard, of that he beareth witness; and no man receiveth his witness. He that hath received his witness hath set his seal to this, that God is true. For he whom God hath sent speaketh the words of God: for he giveth not the Spirit by measure. The Father loveth the Son, and hath given all things into his hand. He that believeth on the Son hath eternal life; but he that obeyeth not the Son shall not see life, but the wrath of God abideth on him.

JOHN 3:22-36

Chapter Eleven

Make Way for Christ!

MARCO POLO in the account of his travels tells of an island people who worship all day long the first object they see each morning. Not so illogical at that! Is not that about what we do too? That which is first and most important in our scale of values is what we see first, think of and worship. Borglum, the famous sculptor, tells how he prepared himself mentally for carving one of his statues. He says: "I saw every known photograph. I read every book about him. I looked up many who had seen him. Then I had my own mental picture and reproduced it." What do we see first and clearest? That we are likely to reproduce.

The most important thing in everybody's life is what he believes. I don't mean what he *says* he believes; I mean what he shows he believes by the way he habitually acts. If a man believes in a bank he puts his money into it. If he believes in a business venture he invests in it. If he believes in a person he trusts him. If you believe in Christ you yield to His direction in all areas of your life.

Let no one protest that beliefs do not matter— that it is only behavior which counts. We behave as we believe. Men were impelled into the air because they believed that air would sustain objects heavier than itself. Adventuresome souls were driven to far corners of the earth because they believed it to be round. Men were burned at the stake for holding beliefs too dangerous for their contemporaries and One went to the cross for what He believed about God and man. What the Nazis did was bound up with what they believed about race and the state. What the Japanese did at Pearl Harbor was the inevitable conclusion of what they believed about the Emperor.

To believe is important. What we believe is equally important. But there is a delicate balance here. "The worst things are corruptions of the best," as the ancient adage has it. If you want to put this more vividly say, "The worst is the rotten best!" Thrift is a fine thing, surely. Corrupt it, and what have you? Miserliness! Prudence and discretion are virtues, but corrupt them and you have timidity, even cowardice. Such a fine thing as courage can be reduced to foolhardiness and rashness. Love, the highest of virtues, corrupted, becomes base and bestial passion and lust.

What is the greatest thing you have in life? If you could be sure about this, presumably that is what you ought to believe in. What is the greatest in your life? Yourself! Your ego, individuality!

Your "I," of course. You use that little word many times a day: "I am; I wish; I think; I shall; I must; I do; I don't; I, I, I." In your letters the capital I's stand out like marching soldiers, reinforced by "me, mine, we, ours."

So it should be; it is a sign of the dignity of man. Animals do not say "I" nor even think "I." Even babies talk first about themselves in the third person—"baby wants this" and "baby wants that"—but with development of conscious unity and selfhood "I want" begins to be heard. Right there begins the corruption of self and the struggle against selfishness. Let us realize it is a wholesome thing for a man to have respect for that self —to have self-respect. We pray with that old Edinburgh weaver, "My God, give me a good conceit of myself!" Exactly! A man ought to have a good opinion of himself. Del Sarto may be pardoned for saying, "I know that I can paint as well as Raphael, and I can paint better than most of my contemporaries." He could, and he knew it, and respected his own ability.

Not against self-respect would I speak, but against selfishness and pride and arrogance. These are not self-respect, but the "I" inflated out of proportion, going crazy, bullying everybody else off the stage.

If ever man was tempted to corrupt the fine thing which ego and individuality are, it was John the Baptist. Our Gospel for today is a particularly sensitive portrayal of this tension. The whole conflict of whether he should get out of the way and let Christ occupy the pre-eminence drew to a dramatic climax and the Baptist was equal to the test.

Remember that John had been quite a figure for this time. He was different; he had color and atmosphere about him. His mode of life evoked curiosity—he was stern and ascetic. He preached strangely too! He had a following both of disciples and hangers-on. It is recounted that whole areas of the countryside came out to listen to him and be baptized by him. All this was not calculated to discount his own estimate of his place in society.

Despite this nourishing of his own ego, we have evidence enough of his bold witness to the Messiah promised of old. He had pointed to Him as the Lamb of God which taketh away the sin of the world. He had likened himself to a voice crying in the wilderness making ready the path of Another. That One, he affirmed, was so much higher than he that he was not worthy to unloose the latchet of His shoes. Had he wished to cultivate his following, John could have been his own messiah. But he got out of the way for The Messiah!

Jesus was in debt to John for his unmistakable witness. And now John's disciples report that this rival whom their own leader had built up by his commendation is stealing the people away from him. "He is baptizing, and all are going to him." What unthinking ingratitude! What a splendid invitation to nurse a grievance! Easily, John's pride and place might have been hurt beyond redemption by such information brought angrily by his own disciples.

John rose above that. He knew his powers and his place. Just exactly what is reported to have happened is what he had labored for. "He must increase, but I must decrease." That is the sum of it all. Consummation had come. What is more, he rejoiced to see it realized: "Therefore this joy of mine is now full."

It is relevant and worthwhile for us to search out how John the Baptist could find such a purposeful and victorious way of using self, his ego, his individuality, his "I." Well, he had come upon two secrets: surrender and forgetfulness! It is a wonderful thing to surrender yourself to another life, to a bigger life. Here's a young man who used to be silly, selfish. He met a girl one day; he fell desperately in love with her. She filled his whole world. He forgot himself and then he woke up to the fact that he still had a self and he ran and laid it at her feet at the altar one day. And she— why, her mother said: "I never saw such a change in my life! My daughter was utterly selfish, thoughtless and inconsiderate till the day she met him. Now she thinks of nobody but that man!"

Genuine Christian belief means this and more. It takes us and says to us, "Surrender to Christ; down on your knees!" That is the surrender of Holy Communion. "All that I am and have I give to Thee. I lift my empty life to Thee; cleanse and redeem it, fill it and use it." The sinner who, in his first attempt to know God, found himself at heaven's gate, pounded on the door, and hearing a voice asking, "Who is there?" answered, "I," but got no reply and gained no entrance. He knocked again and again, and having thought deeply rapped more gently. The voice asked, "Who is there?" and he answered, "Thou!" The gate opened. That is the heart of Christianity.

This surrender is not something of words alone. When the emissaries of Napoleon came to surrender to the Duke of Wellington they complimented him on his brilliant strategy. They were elegant in courtly manner; with many words they flattered him. But enough of this and the Iron Duke broke in sharply: "Gentlemen, your swords!" And Christ said, "Not every one who saith, Lord, Lord, but he who doeth the will of my Father which is in heaven." John's surrender whereby he found victorious use for his "I" was a surrender of an entire life in thought, words and deeds.

And now, forgetfulness. The good football player is lost in the game; playing on the team, watching the ball. Not for him is the indulgence of seeing to it that his helmet is on straight. He is in the game. Soldiers don't pose in battle; they have forgotten all save the whole, the regiment, the cause. John had learned not to pamper self by losing himself, forgetting himself in a consuming devotion. He had found the greatest cause of all in which to forget himself—pointing others to Christ.

Jesus laid down this rule: "He that saveth his own life shall lose it." Keep a seed on your shelf and it will shrivel up. Plant that seed and it bursts into new life and harvest. Your life hoarded and kept will die; invested daringly in the program of Christ it will live and multiply. If I want to save my life I must lose it. John lived by that princi-

ple and experienced the magic of harvest and rejoiced in it. Save your life and you are doomed to
the hell inhabited by those who have lived for
themselves alone. Dante saw them moving about
without pause. They aren't wanted in heaven.
They aren't wanted in hell. The selfish person
is doomed to the hell of living with himself forever and ever.

Legend tells of the baptism of the King of
Munster by Saint Patrick. The crozier of Ireland's
patron saint was spear-pointed at its base, the better to make it stick in the ground as he put it
beside him when he was preaching outdoors. Before administering the Sacrament to the King,
Saint Patrick had jabbed the crozier into the earth,
so that his hands might be free. After the baptism he reached for his crozier and was mortified
to note that he had struck the spear point through
the King's foot and it was bleeding. Upon Saint
Patrick's apologizing for this, the King said, "That
is quite all right; I thought it was part of the baptism." Naive? He had learned something of the
genius of crucifying the self, of surrender, of higher remembrance. Take that capital "I" and cancel
it. What have you got? You have the cross. The
cross is the "I" cancelled.

Let us learn of John concerning that cross and
its pre-eminence and particularly of the pre-eminence of the Christ on that cross. He had something to say about this. "He must increase . . .
He who comes from above is above all." Deep
humility and high adoration such as John exhibits
are requisites for our worthy commemoration of

Christmas. Without these qualities no Christ will be born in us. To prepare us for such holy birth is the purpose of this Advent season and very especially of this last Sunday in Advent.

The finger, luminous with light and vibrant with the angelic Gloria, which pointed down from the Bethlehem sky that first Christmas night was but the ratification of prophetic promise. Upon the world stage in that obscure Palestinian town that night stepped the most conspicuous character of history. It had been foretold; the people should have expected it. But they did not recognize the eternal and universal importance of what was taking place in their midst. It remained for the Christmas carol poet much later to write, "The hopes and fears of all the years are met in thee tonight." Truly this was God's moment of redeeming humility and enlivening majesty.

In many books are stories of the ruler who laid aside royal robes and mingled unrecognized among his people. This theme has infinite possibilities. To a vivid imagination it opens the whole world of adventure and the opportunity to observe all sorts and conditions of men realistically. The sultan feels the thrill of common life!

Different by far is the incarnation of the Son of God. The compassionate Father, yearning over His earthly children, sends into the world His unique Son, to bridge the whole vast gulf between God and man. How could this be done? "He emptied himself, taking the form of a servant, being born in the likeness of men. And being found in human form he humbled himself." So the method is strangely familiar; kingly prerogatives are laid aside and He becomes like the rest. But how about purpose and motive? "God so loved the world that he gave his only begotten Son, that whosoever believeth in him should not perish, but have everlasting life." The purpose is redemptive, and the motive is self-sacrificing love.

Note how God takes steps to meet man on his own ground. The Lord Jesus is born like a man, He lives like a man, He dies like a man, and, most wonderful of all, He rises to eternal life like a man. This is not to say that Christ is not divine. He is. But as we approach Christmas, the festival of His coming in human flesh, is it not thrilling to know how He fills the whole cycle of human possibilities and destiny, standing before our very eyes in transcendent appeal and victory, smiling and holding out His hand to us? God, the Father, in Christ, does all this for us. He has swept everything aside to meet us. Will we not go to meet Him?

Born like a man. "He humbled himself to be born of a virgin." So His birth was of a lowly country maiden, member of a despised and subject race, seeing His first light in the stable of an inn, cradled in a manger borrowed from the ox and ass. Rustics leave their sheep and stand about in awe. There was no room in the hostel; no attention given from the holiday crowd, the elders of Bethlehem or the Roman officials. Suitable for the short and simple annals of the poor, all this. Yet because of Him who thus humbled Himself, all generations have called that maiden blessed, all motherhood and childhood have been ennobled, the humble exalted, the meek inherit the earth, all men have the potential of salvation. No wonder, then, that heavenly hosts give glory to God, and men of wisdom offer their finest gifts, while men of devout heart sing, "Now let thy servant, Lord, depart in peace, for mine eyes have seen thy salvation."

He lives like a man. Presented in the temple with the poor man's offering; smuggled away by night to save His wee life; hidden in an alien land till danger goes; raised in a remote hill village, earning His bread at a carpenter's bench: these are fitting sequel to His humble birth. All His short ministry this was to be cast up to Him. "Can any good thing come out of Nazareth?" "Is not this the carpenter?" He knew the ways of nature, loving the lilies of the field and the fowls of the air. He walked the ways of common men, watching the farmer sow his seed and the fisher cast his net. The rich sneered, "A friend of publicans and sinners"; the fanatic cried, "A Samaritan that hath a devil." All human emotions were His. Jesus wrestled with temptation, blazed with indignation, loved, wept, hungered, rejoiced. He obeyed the laws of God, observed the pious customs of the church and the just demands of the state. He was praised and blamed, loved, misunderstood, slandered. Yet he went everywhere doing good, ministering to every need. He taught with authority which people recognized instinctively. Because of Him men came to love goodness and truth in spite of themselves. They grew to love God because they saw the Father's invincible love in the Son. Hope and faith were born anew, and they became new creatures. Friends called Him Master; the boldest said, "Thou art the Christ."

He dies like a man. Religious bigotry and worldliness conspire to take away His life. His very presence is a silent rebuke to living sin and dead religion. They find a traitor among His closest friends; the rest forsake and flee. His trial is a mockery of justice; witnesses lie, judges are intimidated, the crowd cries for blood. He is insulted, tortured and dragged away to be crucified. And He takes it like a man, using that saying in praise of all that is best in human nature—courage and patience and forgiveness and irresistible faith in the final triumph of right. Manlike, He had dreaded to drink the bitter dregs of death, but He was obedient to the Father's will. In the hour of death He forgives His enemies, saves a dying thief, comforts His mother. He dies and all who will see can know how much God loves the world. Being lifted up, He draws all men unto Him. He could not save Himself, because He wanted to save us. He "became obedient unto death, even the death of the cross."

He rises to eternal life like a man. With tears they seal His body in the grave. The third day His body is not there; He is risen. Jesus Himself comes and stands among them: "It is I . . . Handle me and see; for a spirit hath not flesh and bones, as ye see me have." For forty days He meets them in familiar places, with familiar ways: the very Jesus they have known, yet living a life that is beyond life, a life that has conquered death and time and space and all limitations of mortality. He called this the real life and proclaimed, "Because I live, ye shall live also." They who heard Him then believed that; we believe it. With hands raised in blessing He commands that all men everywhere should be told this good news, promising His own presence always.

These are some of the facts about His life we must have in mind as we go to the work of making the story of Christ known over the world. It is facts like these, some fulfilled then and others not, John the Baptist had in mind when he so effectively magnified the Christ before his disciples that day in our Gospel. "He must increase. . . . He who comes from above is above all."

An old Spanish painter is said to have requested of people that they throw down some bread crumbs on the table and he would proceed to draw a figure around the crumbs. These very bewildering and conflicting days are the crumbs thrown down before us. It calls for a figure to give them shape, direction and meaning. The magazine *Fortune* said at Christmas time last year that that must be the face of Christ. This publication included a portfolio of great art inspired through the ages by the single figure of Christ. Editorially, *Fortune* said: "For untold millions he is the symbol of the compassion of which the modern world stands in need. For Christendom, the Christendom that includes Europe and once included Russia, and from which the New World was born,

Christ stands for more. He stands for the faith that man stems from the divine, and that men must forever treat one another as ends, not means, if they are to build the good society. Perhaps it is the neglect of this heritage that has led modern man into trouble. Perhaps in recapturing these truths there is a way out."

This is "a way out." It is more—it is the only way out! But if He shall be the way out for individuals, for society, for the nation and for the family of nations, we, as John the Baptist did, must get ourselves out of the way for Christ. The winsome Christ on the cross will be manifest to the world only when the domineering "I" is cancelled out by the horizontal of self-less compassion and devotion, rooted in the sturdy vertical of victorious surrender to Christ. "He must increase, but I must decrease." Bending low at the Bethlehem stable manger this Christmas, the prophet long ago phrased what ought to be our approach and attitude: "Wherefore God hath highly exalted him, and given him a Name that is above every name; that at the name of Jesus every knee should bow, and every tongue confess that Jesus Christ is Lord, to the glory of God the Father."

Almighty God, who hast given Thine only Son to be a sacrifice for our sin and an example of godly life; give us grace, that we may always thankfully receive Thy gift and daily endeavor ourselves to follow the blessed footsteps of His most holy life in surrender and forgetfulness of self; through Thy Son, Jesus Christ, our Lord.

AMEN

If I bear witness of myself, my witness is not true. There is another that beareth witness of me; and I know that the witness which he witnesseth of me is true. Ye sent unto John, and he bare witness unto the truth. But I receive not testimony from man: but these things I say, that ye might be saved. He was a burning and a shining light: and ye were willing for a season to rejoice in his light. But I have greater witness than that of John: for the works which the Father hath given me to finish, the same works that I do, bear witness of me, that the Father hath sent me. And the Father himself, which hath sent me, hath borne witness of me. Ye have neither heard his voice at any time, nor seen his shape. And ye have not his word abiding in you: for whom he hath sent, him ye believe not. Search the scriptures; for in them ye think ye have eternal life: and they are they which testify of me.

JOHN 5:31-39 (King James)

Chapter Twelve

That Ye Might Be Saved

THE Advent season is drawing to a close. The glorious Christmas festival is at hand. The prepared hearts will be thrilled with the angelic message, heralding the coming of our Savior, Christ the Lord, and will know the "joy unspeakable and full of glory."

Unfortunately many others are not ready to share in that jubilation. The presence of Christ means as little to them as to those to whom He said, "Ye have neither heard his [the Father's] voice at any time . . . and ye have not his word abiding in you: for whom he hath sent ye believe not." For these, life is empty even at Christmas; for these, we regret to say, eternity will be infinitely worse.

The seeking Shepherd still walks among us. He hears the querulous complaints of those who say: "Is it not too much to expect us to believe in Christ, without credible witnesses?" He lovingly answers with but one purpose in mind. "These things I say that ye might be saved."

The testimony of unimpeachable and trustworthy witnesses clearly and convincingly declares the truth that "Jesus is the way to salvation to all believing souls."

Though Christ is Himself the truth and His Word is truth, yet He does not here testify for Himself. Rather, He calls upon three other witnesses.

In the first place, He presents John the Baptist, "a burning and shining light." Even those who opposed Christ had shown confidence in John, by sending a delegation to him seeking light on spiritual matters (John 1:19 ff). They had rejoiced in his light. Surely his veracity was unquestionable! He was a man of irreproachable character, chosen of God to be a witness for Christ. "And I know that the witness which he witnesseth of me is true," said our Lord.

John has left this testimony that Jesus Christ is not to be compared either with him or with Moses. "Grace and truth came by Jesus Christ. No man hath seen God at any time; the only begotten Son, which is in the bosom of the Father, he hath declared him" (John 1:17-18). Persuasively did this great prophet by the Jordan point to Jesus and urge sinners to "behold the Lamb of God which taketh away the sin of the world" (John 1:29).

Christ needed no supporting word from John for His own sake. "I receive not testimony from man." But the importance of John's message for man was incalculable, for what he said was sufficient for anyone to believe Christ. "These things I say, that ye might be saved."

Since John's day, many a lesser light has burned and shined for Christ. As every true Christian pastor, parent, teacher, neighbor has offered his God-given testimony to Christ, there has been illumination from above. Those who have heard the Gospel from the lips of faithful Christians have had all the evidence needed that they might believe and be saved.

In the second place, our Lord calls forth a "greater witness than that of John." It is a witness in keeping with His own exalted Person. "The works which the Father hath given me to finish, the same works that I do, bear witness of me, that the Father hath sent me."

It was the work of our Lord to live in this sinful world. He faced life realistically. He entered into the everyday affairs of men. He met the different classes of people. He "was in all points tempted like as we are, yet *without sin*" (Heb. 4:15). Never did He yield to a single temptation; never did He deviate from the path of rectitude. From the manger cradle to the Golgotha Cross, Christ lived in perfect harmony with the will of the Father. That work bears witness to Him.

It was the work of our Lord to do good. He did not only what man can do, He performed deeds which only God can do. He healed the one who had been hopelessly sick for thirty-eight years, He cleansed the lepers, gave sight to the blind, hearing to the deaf, speech to the dumb. He made the paralytic walk. He raised the dead. He granted the divine grace of forgiveness of sins to penitent sinners. That blessed ministry of mercy witnesses for Christ.

The witness of the works of Christ is a glorious credential. Time has not impaired this, but rather added luster and honor to it. Scrutinized, attacked, defended, this witness still stands trustworthy and convincing. Ignore it, and it will rise to condemn you on that great Judgment Day. Let it speak to your heart, and it will draw you to the Savior.

The last witness is to be heard. Listen: "And the Father himself which hath sent me, hath borne witness of me. . . . Search the scriptures. . . . They are they which testify of me."

In our Holy Bible we have this witness of the Father. That precious Book is God's revelation to man, for "all scripture is given by inspiration of God" (II Tim. 3:16). From Genesis to Revelation, every book, every chapter, every word is the inspired Word of God. "The words that I speak unto you, they are spirit, and they are life" (John 6: 63).

The Scriptures focus our attention upon One, the Lord Jesus Christ. As has been said,

The Bible has one theme—Law and Gospel, history and prophecy; every part, as well as the completed whole, affirms, defines, and illuminates the one supreme subject. From first to last the Book speaks of Christ and His work —foreshadowed and performed. Thus:

In Genesis, the Seed of the Woman.
In Exodus, the Passover Lamb.
In Leviticus, the Atoning Sacrifice.
In Numbers, the Smitten Rock.
In Deuteronomy, the Prophet yet to come.
In Joshua, the Captain of the Lord's Host.
In Judges, the Great Deliverer.
In Ruth, the Celestial Kinsman.
In the King Books (6), Jesus, Promised King.
In Ezra, Restorer of the Temple.
In Nehemiah, Restorer of the Nation.
In Esther, Advocate and Propitiator.
In Job, "My Redeemer," for patient souls.
In Psalms, My All in All for ardent souls.
In Proverbs, the Pattern for prudent souls.
In Ecclesiastes, the Goal for seeking souls.
In Song of Solomon, the Center of all for loving souls.
In the Prophets, the coming Prince of Peace.
In the Gospels, Christ coming to seek and save.
In the Acts, the risen Christ with His finished work.
In the Epistles, the Christ waiting at God's right hand.
In Revelation, the Christ returning to reign.

The witness for Christ has been perfected
"These are written, that ye might believe that
Jesus is the Christ, the Son of God; and that be-
lieving ye might have life through his name"
(John 20:31).

As we face this three-fold testimony to Christ,
we have a great responsibility. We must make a
decision.

We are in need of the saving grace of God in
Christ. It is indicative of the inborn, deep-seated

perversity of man that God must confront him with such cumulative evidences. We are by nature doubters, and face the holy God with skepticism, if not plain hostility. The creature contends with his Creator! We are helpless in the grip of the mighty forces of sin. Our wills are bound; our hearts are deceptive and desperately wicked; our minds are darkened. No wonder our consciences are disturbed. What poor, lost and condemned sinners we are!

Only God can save us. An almighty power that moves at the call of perfect redemptive love and mercy must reach down to lift us up and restore us to God's favor. The testimony points unerringly and alone to Jesus Christ as that Savior. He is God's all-sufficient answer to the needs of all sinners.

Not for one race or color alone
Was He flesh of your flesh and bone of your bone.
Not for you only—for all men He died,
On the rock, Golgotha, crucified.
Five were the wounds from which He bled,
Five were the colors the angel said,
Yellow, and black, white, brown, and red,
All men redeemed by the thorn-crowned head.

The testimony bids us believe in Jesus Christ as our personal Savior. "Search the scriptures" with an open mind, with a reverent attitude, praying for the light of the Holy Spirit, and you will experience the grace of salvation.

As you face the stern and uncompromising demand, "Repent ye," then listen, and obey. The deep resentment of the unconverted heart simply increases the urgency of immediate surrender. Hard is our heart; it must be broken in penitence. Strong is our resistance; it must be shattered. We must come to realize with sorrow that we are sinners and deserve only the wrath of God. Down so low must we stoop that we can only plead with God for mercy for Jesus' sake.

The glad notes of the Gospel will then be welcome. "Believe on the Lord Jesus Christ, and thou shalt be saved" (Acts 16:31) will be for us a power of God unto salvation. As we hear that precious Gospel promise, we will be enabled to trust in Him as our "only Savior from sin, death and the power of the devil, seek our only refuge in Him and His merits and with intimate confidence rely upon Him." We enter a new world. We are translated into the Kingdom of God's dear Son. We possess eternal life.

He who has accepted the testimony of Christ is blessed. He wonders that anyone should do otherwise. He may well make his own the words:

> I cannot see
> Why men should turn from Thee,
>   My Lord.
> If they could only guess
> Thy matchless loveliness,
> The beauty of Thy face,
> The richness of Thy grace,
>   My Lord.
>
> If they could only see
> Thee on the cruel tree!
> Nor pain nor death was stayed
> Till all our debt was paid,
>   My Lord.

If they could only know
That heart which loves them so,
Their only thought would be
How they might come to Thee,
    My Lord.

The testimony to our Lord Jesus Christ rests now in your hands. Through it He speaks to your heart.

"These things I say, that ye might be saved!"

AMEN

Now it came to pass in those days, there went out a decree from Cæsar Augustus, that all the world should be enrolled. This was the first enrolment made when Quirinius was governor of Syria. And all went to enroll themselves, every one to his own city. And Joseph also went up from Galilee, out of the city of Nazareth, into Judæa, to the city of David, which is called Bethlehem, because he was of the house and family of David; to enroll himself with Mary, who was betrothed to him, being great with child. And it came to pass, while they were there, the days were fulfilled that she should be delivered. And she brought forth her first-born son; and she wrapped him in swaddling clothes, and laid him in a manger, because there was no room for them in the inn. And there were shepherds in the same country abiding in the field, and keeping watch by night over their flock. And an angel of the Lord stood by them, and the glory of the Lord shone round about them: and they were sore afraid. And the angel said unto them, Be not afraid; for behold, I bring you good tidings of great joy which shall be to all the people: for there is born to you this day in the city of David a Saviour, who is Christ the Lord. And this is the sign unto you: Ye shall find a babe wrapped in swaddling clothes, and lying in a manger. And suddenly there was with the angel a multitude of the heavenly host praising God, and saying, Glory to God in the highest, and on earth peace among men in whom he is well pleased.

LUKE 2:1-14

Chapter Thirteen

God's Greatest Gift

THE dominant note of Christmas is that God reveals His grace to man. It is the message from the heavenly throne, sung by the angels, "Unto you is born a Savior."

The heart of Christmas is the birth of the Savior. The festivities, celebrations and rejoicings, whether in community or home, are the human contributions to this great event. The divine element and the eternal is the gift of a Savior to mankind to save from sin and death.

In Luther's hymn the angel sings:

> From heaven above to earth I come
> To bear good news to every home;
> Glad tidings of great joy I bring
> Whereof I now will say and sing.

It is from heaven, from God, that we receive this priceless Christmas gift. We can do without material gifts, without friends and without festivities, but we cannot do without a deliverer from sin. This Savior from sin is God's great gift to mankind.

As John meditates on this deep mystery of God's grace and love, he says: "For God so loved the world, that he gave his only begotten Son, that whosoever believeth in him should not perish, but have everlasting life."

"Unto you is born a Savior," includes the incarnation of God's only begotten Son, His life here on earth, His atoning death on the cross, and His victorious resurrection.

There can be no Christmas, there can be no Savior, if this counsel of God is lacking. That means all the world, not a favored few of one class or one race. The angel said, "Unto all people" and the poet sang, "There's a wideness in God's mercy that is wider than the sea." Today this great mercy and love of God is reaching out to all in His beloved Son.

Why did Jesus Christ come to this world? Why did He become the Child born in the Bethlehem manger? He was truly the Father's only begotten, in the Father's glory. He humbled Himself and took upon Himself the likeness of man and became a servant.

We have often sung the Christmas hymns. We have given each other gifts, and the Christmas candles, with their beaming rays, have lighted our joy. Truly, we can stop and ask: Why did Christ come to the world, as the Christmas Gospel relates? He Himself has given the answer. "The Son of man is come to seek and to save that which was lost." This is the purpose of His coming, to save

the lost, to seek and to find those who had been
separated from the Father by the fall of man,
those who in their hearts had told God farewell.
He came with His grace into humanity and became one with us, in order to reach us and to find
us, who were lost.

This Savior is the Christ, the eternal Son of
God, that became flesh and dwelt among men. He
reveals the Father unto men. No man has ever
seen the Father but the only begotten Son, who
is in His bosom, has declared Him. It is not
strange the angels declared: "Fear not." The
crushing bondage and weight of sin and despair
have been lifted and taken away by the promise of
God in Christ, reconciling the world to Himself.
A great joy has come into the world in the long-
awaited Savior.

The church's chant in each morning service is
the angelic salutation of Christmas, "Glory to God
in the highest." The hope of humanity, the
foundation for faith and trust in God as our
Father, centers in the tremendous mystery that
took place when God became flesh in the Child
born of the virgin.

From the manger in Bethlehem flows the grace
of God to all men. The Christmas Gospel says,
"Good tidings of great joy, which shall be to all
people." All are included in the possibility of
salvation. The marvelous thing in God's grace is
this, that when God loves, when God sends His
Son, there is no exception. There is no respect of
persons. All are included. All are sinners and all
are the objects of God's great mercy and love.

"Unto all people." There are probably some who have hidden themselves away, dug themselves deeply into their own thoughts and own minds, possibly thinking they are not included in this. Yet to such a one comes the mighty calling grace of God. It comes to you, who have considered yourself outside the circle of God's love. Many a lonesome pilgrim walks the streets of the city on Christmas Eve and beholds the Christmas lights and the Christmas joy that pours out through the windows in the different homes. He is lonely. He is cold. He is without friends. Yet God's grace and love are there for him. "For all people." The Child that was born and the Savior that is given brings joy and light and happiness, even to those who sit in darkness.

The Christmas Gospel goes from Judea and Samaria to Greece and Rome, to the uttermost parts of the earth, so that today they are singing Christmas hymns in Madagascar, China, Africa, South America—the world over. All are included, the greatest sinner as well as the noblest of men. All have need of God's grace in Jesus Christ.

"Peace on earth," the angels sang. These words sound strange to our ears as the thunder of the cannons has stopped on the battlefields of the world and men are yet groping for peace. There are still bitterness and hatred in the hearts of men; yet the Christmas message calls "Peace on earth."

The Child born in the manger came to bring peace on earth and good will among men. He is truly the Prince of Peace. He came, not up from humanity, but from God to us and became one

with us. If we are to have true peace on earth
there must be peace in our own hearts, peace
through the forgiveness of sins, through the acceptance of a Savior from our sins.

"From heaven above to earth I come." But man
seeks peace and lasting happiness of his own making and so there comes no lasting peace. It is only
in the peace of God, peace like a river that comes
from his Savior, that there will be peace in the
heart of man and peace for humanity.

A great joy! Dare we think of joy today, many of
us? There is much sorrow, suffering and pain in
the world. There are so many broken plans, so
many blasted hopes that it is strange to talk about
joy. There are millions today for whom there is
little joy, and yet a great joy is being given us in
the Christ child. It comes to each of us—to me
when He becomes my Savior, when I can place my
burden of sin and my broken life at His feet.
When I can kneel as a child before the manger in
Bethlehem He becomes my Savior, He who came
to seek and save that which was lost.

The Christmas Gospel, the drawing power of
God's grace and Holy Spirit, clears the hindrances
for you and for me to take Him truly into our
own lives.

We sang as little children:

> Thy little ones, dear Lord, are we,
> And come Thy lowly bed to see;
> Enlighten every soul and mind,
> That we the way to Thee may find.

So we come as little ones of His and find in His
word of life and in His promises the assurance for

that peace which comes to lives whose sins are forgiven through this Savior who was born in Bethlehem.

God's greatest gift—how much more glorious than all earthly gifts! He can be mine, He can become yours. We say with the shepherds: "Let us now go even unto Bethlehem, and see this thing which is come to pass."

We need not cross the great oceans and travel to distant lands. We need not make a long pilgrimage as did the wise men of old. He is close to us. In the very Word of life which He has given; in the very Gospel which we have heard —Jesus comes to you and to me.

From the lowly village church to the great city cathedral, from Christian lands as well as from foreign fields today, the song arises, "Glory be to God, for unto us a Savior is born."

Christmas is Christ. It can never be anything else. Without Christ Christmas is a hollow mockery. The entire world in its reckoning of time calls each year *Anno Domini,* the year of our Lord. It is the center, the heart of life for the world, the birth of Jesus Christ in Bethlehem on that first Christmas day.

> To you this night is born a Child
> Of Mary, chosen mother mild;
> This little Child, of lowly birth,
> Shall be the joy of all the earth.
>
> 'Tis Christ, our God, who far on high
> Hath heard your sad and bitter cry;
> Himself will your salvation be,
> Himself from sin will make you free.   AMEN

And his father and his mother were marvelling at the things which were spoken concerning him; and Simeon blessed them, and said unto Mary his mother, Behold this child is set for the falling and rising up of many in Israel; and for a sign which is spoken against; yea and a sword shall pierce through thine own soul; that thoughts out of many hearts may be revealed. And there was one Anna, a prophetess, the daughter of Phanuel, of the tribe of Asher (she was of a great age, having lived with a husband seven years from her virginity, and she had been a widow even unto fourscore and four years), who departed not from the temple, worshipping with fastings and supplications night and day. And coming up at that very hour she gave thanks unto God, and spake of him to all them that were looking for the redemption of Jerusalem. And when they had accomplished all things that were according to the law of the Lord, they returned into Galilee, to their own city Nazareth. And the child grew, and waxed strong, filled with wisdom: and the grace of God was upon him.

LUKE 2:33-40

Chapter Fourteen

They Knew Him

FROM the first clear notes sounded five weeks ago by the bugles of the Advent heralds and from the first thrilling words of the Advent chant, "Behold thy King cometh unto thee," our hearts have been caught and held by the dramatic story of the entrance of the Son of God into human experience. As the anthem of the angel chorus, "Glory to God in the highest and on earth peace," became again a wondrous reality, we found ourselves joining our voices to the ecstatic Christmas hymns, "Joy to the World, the Lord Is Come," "Hark the Herald Angels Sing," "Rejoice, Rejoice This Happy Morn." Our hearts have been lifted and our lives refreshed by the radiance which Christmas always brings. We have needed music and praise, pageant and gayety to give expression to what we have felt. Of course we remember that it wasn't that way the first Christmas—not in Bethlehem. When the echoes of the angel song had died away on the dark hillsides, the awe-struck shepherds went to David's city with strange unspoken questions. When Mary and Joseph heard the shepherds' halting story, they kept these things within themselves, not speaking openly to anyone. It was truly a "Silent night, holy night, all is calm," "O little town of Bethlehem, how still we see thee lie." Too still! Too calm! There should have been a celebration.

A baby boy had been born. God's Son, the Savior, had come unto His own. There should have been a call for musicians. The village ought to have been aroused and the town-crier sent along each street pounding on doors, shouting, "Awake, arise! The Christ, the Messiah, He for whom we have waited a thousand years has come." A runner should have been dispatched to speed the news to Jerusalem and the quickly gathered crowd ought to have chanted, "Hallelujah. God has visited His people!"

But it was "Silent night" . . . "All is calm" . . . "how still." Too still! For all except the angels, the shepherds and Mary and Joseph it was just another night. The people didn't know what had happened. They didn't know that Christ had come.

Sweet little Jesus Boy—they made You be born in a
    manger.
Sweet little Holy Child we didn't know who You wuz.
Didn't know You'd come to save us, Lawd
To take our sins away:
Our eyes was blind, we couldn't see
We didn't know who You wuz.

A few days after the child Jesus was born, Mary and Joseph brought Him to the temple. There they found two Spirit-filled people who knew who He was and who, because of their knowledge, "blessed God" and "gave thanks to God." As Simeon held the child Jesus in his arms and Anna stood by, they could praise and glorify God for they knew that the age-long promises of God had been fulfilled.

Yet as they stood there, the marvel of it was not so much that a promise had been kept as that God was willing to become *man* and be a Savior for the people Israel. That is what amazed them most as it did the Apostle Paul later. He spoke often of the fact that God loved us when we deserved no love, that even though the Israelites were obstinate, rebellious and seemingly indifferent to His will, He loved them anyway and sent His Son to redeem them. As these two old saints, Simeon and Anna, thought of this and tried to measure the greatness, the goodness and the magnificence of it, they could only bless God and give Him thanks.

Because, you see, if any of us had been in God's place and looked at the evil, twisted world He had to see, with not much good in it any more, we should not have been too eager to do what God did. "If I were God," said a famous man one day, "if I were God and the world had treated me as it treated Him, I think I'd have kicked the wretched thing to pieces long ago." That's likely the way we'd feel about it, at first anyway.

Just suppose you had been God. Suppose that

in one mighty act of love you had molded the
universe and made man in your own image. Try
to think what would have happened to you had
you gone through those creative processes so beautifully described by James Weldon Johnson in his
poem, "The Creation." He pictures God making
His world and finding, when He was finished, that
He was lonely in the midst of all He had created.

> Then God sat down . . .
> With His head in His hands.
> God thought and thought
> Till He thought, "I'll make me a man."
> Up from the bed of the river,
> God scooped the clay,
> And by the bank of the river
> He kneeled Him down:
> And there the great God Almighty
> Who lit the sun and fixed it in the sky,
> Who flung the stars to the most far corner
>   of the night—
> This great God,
> Like a mammy bending over her baby
> Kneeled down in the dust,
> Toiling over a lump of clay,
> Till He shaped it in His own image;
> Then into it He blew the breath of life,
> And man became a living soul.

Suppose *you* had done that and then after
awhile were forced to see what you had so tender-
ly fashioned become ugly and distorted from its
first glory and purpose, had seen your own creation shake its puny fist in your face and insist that
its twisted wisdom was greater than your own,
what would you have been tempted to do?

God could have given up on men. Quit cold.
Or let the human race be destroyed by its own

folly. But He didn't! Instead He set a star in the
sky and an angel chorus in the heavens and came
in Christ to win men back to Himself, to give
back to mankind the spiritual heritage they had
wasted. That was the wonder of it long ago to
those who knew who He was. That is still the
marvel of Christ's coming—to those who know
Him.

How the world of Simeon and Anna needed
what they knew that Child was to bring. How we
need it now!

We need what Christ can bring because the
world is a sad world and Christ's coming is characterized by song. In the shadow of a great and
terrible war, three things stand like ghostly
specters beside us: the dead, the wretched, and the
bomb. These are the inescapable realities of our
time. At Nürnberg the trial of the German war
criminals has unfolded a story of death and in-
humanity that is incomprehensible. Millions of
people were destroyed because of their race or
religion. Millions of sons will no longer wend their
way home for Christmas, not because of the press
of business or crowded trains but because they
sleep in battle graveyards the sleep of the warrior
dead.

Over the hollow echo of political scheming and
double talk we are hearing a more awesome sound,
the piteous cries of children who are denied a
slice of bread. The humanitarian leaders of the
world are pleading for a return of a tender conscience to the world so that the ravages of famine
and disease may be checked—in time.

Sadness and fear! And over all, the threat of atomic power which may yet be the ruin of what we have built. We'd like to laugh when school-girls in great cities wish to leave school for fear of being destroyed by a possible attack on their city, but the laughter won't come somehow, because we know it can happen. It's a sad world, without much joy.

It was that when a little boy was born in Bethlehem. It was sadder then because there was no Christmas with its songs of hope. The world was not sure that God was interested in it any more. A few guessed that He might be, but it looked as though He had forgotten the man He had made because He was Himself lonely. But since that first Christmas the world has seen how much God cares. God loves us in spite of what we have done. In a world as gloomy as is ours, what a conviction! He cares enough to participate in our joys and sorrows, enough to come down and enter into our life. My Christ tells me, as He rests in Simeon's arms, that God loves this world of foolish men, that He is a Father to His children. Christ tells us that just by being here.

There was a time, not too many years ago, when that did not mean much to most people. Men's minds would have spoken scornfully, "We do not want God's love and care. We do not need it. We are full-grown men and can take care of ourselves; as Heine used to boast, 'We are not children.'"

But that was before chaos broke in upon us. That was when this universe of ours seemed manageable. Now security is gone and the future holds grim possibilities. So in a strange, dangerous and uniquely unfamiliar world, it makes a mighty difference to know that there is One who never forgets us. It enables us to lift our voices in happy song. The angels were right when they sang jubilantly, "Glory to God in the highest." The medieval man had a reason for his song, "Now sing we, now rejoice, now raise to heaven our voice." Modern people too have cause for meaning it when they sing, "Joy to the world, the Lord is come." Just as Anna did when she gave thanks unto God.

We need what Christ can bring because the world is dark and Christ's coming is characterized by radiance and brightness. To say that the world is stumbling in darkness is to state a commonplace. Though the lights are beginning to come on here and there, it is still a place of shadows. But Christ in Simeon's arms is ever a light and a glory "prepared before the face of all peoples." God is here with men in Christ. Wherever He is there are no blackouts of life or of hope. He is a light in darkness, the Morning Star which, since the shepherds first saw Him, has been shining. No circumstance, no tragedy, no grief, no sin, no person, no nation, can ever put that light out.

A writer recently reminded us of the young Nazi who said to his mother ten years ago, "Mother, Adolf Hitler is getting so big and Jesus Christ is getting so little." In certain places on occasion men try to put out the radiance which Christ has brought, but the light is dimmed only briefly. For ten years later that same German lad, if he is alive, may be saying, "Hitler has shrivelled to nothing but Christ is getting big." All of us realize, I suppose, as never before in our lifetime, that this Man of Nazareth has outlived all the mighty ones who mocked Him. At all events a generation is coming into being at last that is turning with hope to religion and which is conscious of the fact that the only brightness we have comes from it. Luther said it long ago,

> The eternal light to us descends,
> Its brightness to the earth it lends,
> And purely shines upon our night
> To make us children of the light.

In a college town two men were walking home one evening when one of them pointed to a light which burned brightly on the highest point of one of the college buildings, a light which could be seen from everywhere in town. He said to his friend, "I hope they never put that light out. It helps me more than I can describe. When I'm tired or discouraged, somehow it gives me courage and renewed hope." As long as the radiance of Christ is with us, and that will be forever, men will have a place to turn for courage and for power over despair. Maybe that was in the mind of a Denver woman, a few years ago, who knew she had only a few days to live. She was asked if there was any special thing she'd like. Her home faced the city square where she could see workmen putting up the community Christmas decorations. She said, "I'd like to see the Christmas lights once more." On December 16 they were turned on for one Denver woman so that in an hour of darkness she might see the lights of Christmas. It seems to me we all have sought the same help ever since God "lit the East and Hope was born."

We need what Christ can bring because our world is terribly complex and Christ's coming is characterized by simplicity. Modern life becomes so frightfully involved. An advertisement declares, "It takes 29,000 parts to make a bomber." That's a machine so complex that a novice would get lost in a tangle of wires and struts. Present day living is like that, isn't it? We rush around trying to make life better by gadgets and treaties and wars and threats and power and money until the whole business becomes complicated and bewildering.

Then we hear a message from the temple, "This child is set for . . . the rising up of many." Men shall be lifted into new life and walk a new way, the way of meekness, of humility, of justice, love and unselfishness. Men can't laugh that off any longer. He who proclaimed it has been a sign spoken against and a divider between the lost and the saved. But His way is what is most needed now by this tough, cruel world. People who don't believe it sense it now. As the editor of a much read magazine wrote, "The idea of humility and service has been lived out in one great life. It has started now and nothing can stop it. Twenty centuries after Jesus lived in it, the world at last knows that it has just two choices—Christ or chaos." Men are not to be beasts but sons. Men are not to be brutes but brothers. Christmas tells us that if we will give God a chance, life will work out that way. Then our confusion and dismay will disappear. That is redemption given in its simplest terms. It was brought in the simplest way—a little town, a quiet night, a cattle shed, a manger, a baby.

We need what Christ can bring because the world is lost and Christ's coming is characterized by salvation. How to give almighty God His chance is the final problem of life. How to become brothers! How to know that God is our Father! Men have walked many pathways and trod many trails to find an answer to that problem. Then the Child of Mary comes to offer His special gift, salvation. He comes to give us His wisdom, His strength, forgiveness and peace. He offers us Himself as the Way, the Truth and the Life, the One by whom men come to the Father, the One whose blood makes atonement for our sins, the One in whom men of faith have an eternal fellowship.

The kneeling shepherds tell us that our hearts must be humble, expectant and eager, if God is to reveal Himself to us and bestow upon us His grace. Anna and Simeon tell us that if God's Holy Spirit enlightens us we shall not only know the Savior but be enabled to receive Him and be eager to serve Him.

As we receive Him, we learn to serve Him, befriending God's children in a way that really works. For God lifts us to His level and empowers us to do what we could never have done by ourselves. This is salvation indeed.

Dr. Olaf Malmin, editor of *Lutheran Herald,* told of visiting with an army chaplain. At one

point the chaplain said, "There are two things
I've learned so that I'll never forget them."

"What are they?"

"The first is that the greatest thing in the world
is forgiveness of sins—salvation in Christ."

"And the other?"

"The other is that I've got to do something
about it—to be a true brother to my fellowmen."

The world needs what Christ can bring—the
songs of hope, the radiance and glory, the simplicity of purpose and the great word of salvation.
Because of God's unspeakable gift in Christ we
still dare to lift our faces to heaven and let our
hearts hope beyond these twisted times. With
Anna and Simeon of old our lives are caught up
by such a glad certainty that with them we bless
God, giving thanks forever unto Him who sent
His Son to be born in a manger on Christmas Day.

AMEN

And behold, there was a man in Jerusalem, whose name was Simeon; and this man was righteous and devout, looking for the consolation of Israel: and the Holy Spirit was upon him. And it had been revealed unto him by the Holy Spirit, that he should not see death, before he had seen the Lord's Christ. And he came in the Spirit into the temple: and when the parents brought in the child Jesus, that they might do concerning him after the custom of the law, then he received him into his arms, and blessed God, and said, Now lettest thou thy servant depart, O Lord, according to thy word, in peace; for mine eyes have seen thy salvation, which thou hast prepared before the face of all peoples; a light for revelation to the Gentiles, and the glory of thy people Israel.

LUKE 2:25-32

Chapter Fifteen

And the Holy Spirit
Was Upon Him

JOSEPH saddled the donkey early. The work was done with a light heart, for now the substance of faith had been redeemed with the coin of fact. The last time Joseph had saddled the animal for a trip he was preparing to leave Nazareth with his betrothed who was carrying a child. When this had first come to his attention, anger and resentment took hold of him; but before he could say anything to her, an angel appeared to him in a dream. The angel had told him that Mary was with child by the Holy Spirit and that the child was to be given the name Jesus. Then the angel added, ". . . He will save his people from their sins."

After the dream Joseph laid aside his resentment and treated Mary with love and consideration. But his conduct was a venture in faith. And faith was not without its burden. In the quiet hours of the night Joseph wondered much about what was to be. How would he know this child to be what the angel had promised? What would identify Him and His mission?

Now everything was different. The child had been born. The story of the shepherds on the evening of His birth had explained many things and had redeemed the dream experience from being dissipated in doubt.

Forty days had slipped by since Jesus' birth. It was time to present the child in the Temple and to make the redemption offering required by the Law. A burnt offering and a sin offering must also be made for Mary, the mother. Joseph prepared for the trip to Jerusalem with a song on his lips. God pays off with a singing heart whenever His children obey His leading.

Joseph and Mary found the Temple a busy place. There were others who had come on similar missions. But they saw no one whom they knew. They felt tired and alone among so many strange faces. While they were making arrangements for the sacrifices, an old man stood near and watched them intently. He came closer and listened to their conversation. Suddenly he stepped up to inquire if he might hold the child in his arms. A strange light came into his face as Mary handed him the child, and he burst out in a paean of praise:

Lord, now lettest thou thy servant depart in peace, according to thy word;
for mine eyes have seen thy salvation
which thou hast prepared in the presence of all peoples,
a light for revelation to the Gentiles,
and for glory to thy people Israel.

Joseph and Mary marvelled. A new depth was added to the joy that had so recently come into their lives.

We don't know more of Simeon than what Luke tells us in the compass of eleven verses. But in a few quick strokes he has etched for us a character so warm and inviting that Simeon becomes also one of our friends.

Luke announces, "Now there was a man in Jerusalem, whose name was Simeon." Surely, there were many other Simeons in the Judean capital. But perhaps this old friend of God was not only identified but also described by his name. Scripture has a preference for such double duty in the use of names.

The word *Simeon* connotes *favorable hearing*. In all likelihood Luke intends to tell us that here was a man who had grown old in the practice of giving God's word a *favorable hearing*.

From this practice a given set of character traits had emerged in the life of Simeon. They were quickly recognized by those who came to know him. Luke singles them out: ". . . this man was righteous and devout, looking for the consolation of Israel, and the Holy Spirit was upon him." What a biographical summation! In one sweeping statement there is laid before us a man's mode of action, his attitude, the horizons which beckon him, and the power that keeps him in the walk toward the future.

This man was righteous. It is clear that in these words Luke is not describing a condition of achieved perfection. It is rather a description of

Simeon's mode of action in the conscious choices of life.

It doesn't take much imagination to see Simeon in the role of a merchant, a farmer, a carpenter, or a scribe. Whenever he had financial dealings with other men, Simeon was scrupulously honest. Widows and the dispossessed knew him as a friend. Strangers and Gentiles who came to Jerusalem found Simeon a willing helper. For had he not given ear to the word of Jehovah: "He hath shewed thee, O Man, what is good; and what doth the Lord require of thee, but to do justly, and to love mercy, and to walk humbly with thy God."

Simeon could not make sense out of these words without practicing what they implied. And men recognized that he was controlled by this practice. They began to talk about him—but always as one who loved righteous conduct.

". . . this man was righteous *and devout*." To be devout and to be devoted are the same thing with one exception: the word devout defines also the object of devotion. One may be devoted to many human values; but when devotion is directed Godward, we know it as devoutness.

Somewhere, sometime in the life of Simeon there had been a response to God's goodness that had become the controlling decision in his life. He had chosen "to remember his Creator," and in that response he had found God's salvation. Thereafter his primary devotion was to God. He became a devout man.

Simeon was "looking for the consolation of Israel," Luke tells us. Life feeds upon the anticipations that have captured our imaginations. Without such dream tissue in our thought life, living deteriorates into mere existence. There must be horizons that beckon. "Where there is no vision, the people perish."

The tragedies of life are often defined by the lack of quality in the dreams that possess us. All too often our dreams never rise above the level of purely materialistic considerations: upping the balance in the bank pass book, shrewd buying on the stock market, increasing the farm's acreage, wearing smart clothes. And for some, dreams never get above the stomach's level; all anticipations are localized in the Saturday evening binge. But Simeon had anchored his dreams in the Sabbath— and he carried its climate with him throughout the week. He lived in a daily expectancy of the coming of the Messiah. He was "looking for the consolation of Israel."

All devout Jews were Messiah-conscious. Many had lived in the anticipation of seeing the Day Star from on High. Generation after generation had been gathered to the fathers without seeing their beckoning horizon come near. All this Simeon knew, but he did not surrender to any incipient skepticism. He nursed his hope and lived in its power. Then one day a strange conviction stole into his heart. It was as though someone had promised that death would not overtake him until he had seen the Lord's Christ. The idea took hold of his thinking so forcibly that he could not other than identify it as a Spirit-given conviction

It seemed natural for Simeon to connect this promise with the Temple. And one morning when he rose to give himself to prayer, a Voice whispered, "This is the day." Immediately he prepared to go up to the Temple. He was attracted to Mary and Joseph as soon as his eyes fell on the child Mary carried. When he heard the conversation of the parents and a mention of the child's name, he felt sure. It was then that he stepped forth and asked for permission to hold the baby.

Luke records that Joseph and Mary marveled at the words of Simeon when he held the child. They listened and wondered. Today we read and wonder. Where did Simeon get the insight that his words reveal? His eyes saw only a six-weeks-old baby, but his spirit grasped the child's destiny and the significance of His mission.

Listen to the words of Simeon:

. . . for mine eyes have seen thy salvation
which thou hast prepared in the presence of all peoples.

In these words he makes the child and salvation synonymous. Here there is already a predication of the words of our Lord with which we have become so familiar:

I am the bread of life; he who comes to me shall not hunger, and he who believes in me shall never thirst.

I am the door; if any one enters by me, he will be saved, and will go in and out and find pasture.

I am the good shepherd. The good shepherd lays down his life for the sheep.

I came that they might have life, and have it abundantly.

I am the resurrection and the life; he who believes
in me, though he die, yet shall he live, and whoever lives
and believes in me shall never die.

He who has seen me has seen the Father.

As the substance of a tree's foliage lies hidden
in the swelling buds of early spring, so these af-
firmations of our Lord seem wrapped up in Simeon's confession

He speaks of the Messiah as a salvation God has
prepared *in the presence of all peoples*. Simeon's
God was not a national deity. Jehovah was for him
the God of history who had been at work where
all people could see. From the first promise in
the Garden to the proclamation of the prophets,
God had been active preparing a fulness of time.
And now that fulness was at high noon. God had
come into history; He had clothed Himself in
man's body.

Simeon's doxology says of the child Jesus: He
shall be a "light for the revelation to the Gentiles." A light for the Gentiles! Here is a teaching
that leaps forward with full-blown New Testament meaning. There were no contemporaries
who saw that far. All were bogged down in waiting for a political Messiah. Herod and his scribes
trembled lest Jesus might begin a new dynasty.
The five thousand who were fed with five loaves
and two fish could not forget the experience of
that feeding. It held them fast, and He who was
the Bread of Life remained for them a loaf of
bread. And so they wanted to "take him by force
to make him king." Even the faithful eleven
had a difficult time shaking the clay off their feet.

On the very day of Jesus' ascension they hopefully asked, "Lord, will you at this time restore the kingdom to Israel?" Above these earthly conceptions of the Messiah soars the insight of Simeon until it seems as lofty as the blue of the heavens. He discerned in Mary's child a light, a light to lighten the Gentiles.

Every man has needed that Light. God alone knows how many paths there are on which we need illumination. With Cain of old we cover up a weakness with envy and anger. Who is there who has not stood with King Saul in some act of disobedience, evading God's higher ground? Evil is condoned with a careless shift in language that makes passion love, and license freedom. Standards slip from us because we count all things relative. We look out upon a world that is mired in suffering, and wonder why others cannot be as provident as we Americans are. For all such thinking there is only one explanation: we have been standing too far from the Light, lost in the darkness of our own self-sufficiency.

Where does this last Sunday of this year of our Lord find you and me? Are we poking about in the twilight of our own wisdom, throwing sops to conscience whenever it objects? Has our devotion during the year been to God or to many little gods of our own making? Do our best friends have any doubt about whether we love righteousness? What "consolation" are we looking for in the New Year?

Let us not in these last hours of the year set about to do another repair job. The breaches of the soul cannot be made whole with a little glue or solder. Cast yourself upon your God, for He cares for you.

As a father pitieth his children, so the Lord pitieth them that fear him.

Though your sins be as scarlet, they shall be as white as snow.

Ho, every one that thirsteth, come ye to the waters, and he that hath no money; come ye, buy, and eat.

It was in response to a God who offered such promises that Simeon had found his salvation. In unreserved trust, the joy of forgiven sin had flooded his soul. Thenceforth his devotion was fixed upon God, and righteousness became the guideline in his actions. Luke sums it all up with the words, "the Holy Spirit was upon him."

Shall we take our stand on Simeon's tested ground? I know of no greater good that I could wish for you in these last days of the old year. Beloved co-workers in God's vineyard, I pray that the Holy Spirit may be upon you, now and forevermore!

We come to Thee, O Son of Man, for without Thee we are lost in darkness. In Thy light we see light. Keep us ever on the path of Thy holy will. Let the warmth of Thy love energize and sustain us. We pray in Thine own Name.

AMEN

Blessed be the Lord the God of Israel, for he has cared for his people and wrought them redemption; he has raised up a strong saviour for us in the house of his servant David—as he promised of old by the lips of his prophets—to save us from our foes and from the hand of all who hate us, to deal mercifully with our fathers and to be mindful of his holy covenant, of the oath he swore to Abraham our father, that, freed from fear and from the hand of our foes, we should worship him in holiness and uprightness.

LUKE 1:68-75 (MOFFATT)

Chapter Sixteen

Some Practical Lessons
for After-Christmas

OUR text today is the first and longest of the
two sharply defined sections of the *Benedictus*. This hymn of praise was so named because of
the more or less routine procedure in the early
Church of accepting the first word in the Latin
version as the title. It is a glorious song of thanks-
giving, worthy to stand, as it has for hundreds of
years, in the ordered daily worship of the Christian community as an integral part of Matins.
That fact alone can flapjack even the most inert
materialist into the kingdom of dreamers. For it
is indeed an unimaginative and stubbornly tor-
pid soul that fails to see here the reverent people
of every generation finding in this song fit expression for the age-old desire to praise and worship
"the Lord God, who is and was and is coming,
the almighty." "Faith of our fathers, living still,"
we joyously sing, and catch a glimpse of that great
host who, because they were faithful, are clothed

in white. Then and there we become part and
parcel of eternity. We almost forget our mortality
in the warm assurance that we are in this thing,
too, that

> . . . . on earth hath union,
> With God, the Three in One,
> And mystic sweet communion
> With those whose rest is won:

and that is what the *Benedictus* also can and does
do for the Church, whose roots are deep as eternity. Listen to the words again. You will see plainly, I think, what I mean.

> Blessed be the Lord the God of Israel,
> for he has cared for his people and wrought
>   them redemption;
> he has raised up a strong saviour for us
> in the house of his servant David—
> as he promised of old by the lips of his prophets—
> to save us from our foes and from the hand of
>   all who hate us.

Do you not agree that we are infinitely the
richer because we have had this hymn of thanks-
giving as part and parcel of our heritage? We
ought to thank God for Zechariah, that is certain—
thank Him for using his pliable tongue and willing lips to furnish us with something as articulate
and beautiful and meaningful as this Song of
Matins. Zechariah blessed the Church with his
words and graceful meter, enriched civilization
with a work of art that vibrates with life and
meaning. "Filled with the holy Spirit," as Scripture says, he managed to combine the fragile and
exquisite beauty of poetry and the solid and sub-

stantial significance of a fact, an event. Here is happily wedded truth and beauty—a very important matter, as you shall see.

It is Christmastide, truly a season of beauty! It means the haunting charm of the melodious carol; the intriguing mystery of candle-light; the breathful beauty of gaily bedecked trees; myriad and gay garlands, wreaths and flowers; exciting home-comings and gifts and parties. That is one thing. Quite another thing is the sober and factual event of a birth: Christ's. Here, then, just in this season, appear truth and beauty. This is significant because whenever these two appear there emerges, as if upon signal, an ancient and sinister foe of both: a question—the problem of how to effect a satisfactory union. They must be united, and they are madly in love with each other. But, like every thrilling tale of romance, there are obstacles. The chief obstacle is the question of who is to rule the household.

Zechariah's skill in bringing these two together in good comradeship is a skill we ought to master. Our clumsy and awkward attempts and failures today are in no small measure responsible for "the predicament of modern man." Zechariah's success was due to a simple formula. He started right; he started with truth. Thus, for him, the problem was settled by firmly and insistingly enthroning truth as lord and sovereign over beauty. Nor did that mean the decease of beauty. Truth would have been the first to mourn! No, truth loves beauty! But there must also here be strict adherence to a right order of precedence. Such was the skill of this old, inspired priest of the Temple, he knew the fundamental law that gives lordship to truth. And from truth to beauty is a fairly simple matter. Truth knows and woos beauty—truth serves faithfully as a competent critic and guide. Mark well, though, that trouble always dogs the footsteps of him who would give beauty first prize, and first place in making and finding life.

So it comes to pass that Zechariah and his *Benedictus* stand as a stern thundersmith, hurling anathemas at all who would upset the order of things as they are. For instance, Christmas always provides us with the spectacle of a certain proportion of humanity hard at work enjoying the beauty of this great Festival. They insist rather heatedly that the extravagant style and lavish beauty are worthwhile even though divorced from the *event* of Christmas. It is our folly that posed beauty and mood should bewitch us into thinking that frail beauty can stand on her own pretty feet. Thus easily are we led astray! The *event* is only tolerated—even debased. We begin to think in terms of unreality and fable. Christmas, good friends, is more than a temporary refuge from a scowling and hard-fisted world. Christmas is more than an aery flight into the stratosphere of vagarious imagination. Christmas is, and first of all, a solid fact. That fact is our best hope.

Confused as modern man is at this point of Christmas, it becomes rather easy to see how that confusion carries over into other areas of life. As we apply it to such areas, as I hope we all will, it becomes clear that contemporary culture has sold its birthright for a slogan: "art for art's sake." The absurdity of such a claim is finally becoming apparent in the excesses that it has brought in its train. Far too often, its advocates have found their deepest satisfactions in esthetic thrills, made their goals nothing more than relaxation and entertainment, and made their way toward their ultimate by startling sensationalism and vulgar sensuality.

Man's ideas of beauty, left as independent and free from truth (or made ruler of truth), always degenerate into the sensate and crude and meaningless. This becomes clear when we take the time to examine what, under such circumstances, can happen to such a noble and exalted and influential area as that wherein man strives to express himself through painting and drawing. In *I Would Be Private*, Rose Macaulay gives us a description of John Stowe at work.

It was a clear sun-lit day, the boats were setting their fish pots. John Stowe sits before his canvas in the shadow of the woods idly observing the scene. But he was not painting any of its objects but letting them soak into his soul, there to mix themselves together and later emerge in the shape of John Stowe's special version of reality. These images he would try to paint. They would depict, or suggest, the essence of truth. To be sure, it would be only John Stowe's truth. But, as he would argue, isn't that all the truth there is—just my truth and your truth? Having closed his eyes, and opened them, he began to draw rapidly what he had seen in that dark brief flash of the soul. He sketched a number of round, long triangular shapes lying in a row on a beach; some of the objects looked like skulls; some like cast-off limbs from the human body; and others like bottles. Wild pawpaws and cactus sprouted out of some of the skulls. But John suspected himself of doing too much conscious arranging, so he erased the vegetation sprouting from one of the skulls, and put on it a woman's hat with a bird of paradise in it. This pleased him much better, and it struck him that the picture would be called *Woman and the Putrefying Owl*.[1]

In strict fairness it must be said that this is undoubtedly a grotesque caricature of even radically liberal "modern" art, but let us not forget, either, that it comes much closer to portraying our plight than most of us care to admit. All down the line there is need for the admonition that fiction gives us from the lips of the old trader in Havana who says to young Anthony Adverse: "You are a type . . . You have not yet made up your mind what the world is like or what you are . . . and unless you come to some conclusions about yourself and the world, you will be a mere wanderer."[2] The unvarnished fact is, you see, that no truly great persons or people can arise until they reach conclusions about things that are. Until they find truth, they are impotent to create beauty or become benefactors of humanity.

The preacher's task, this first Sunday after Christmas, is clear and dictated. He is not to do as the preacher of the Great Church of Santo Spirito where thousands came in those days before the Reformation for spiritual help, and where Fra Mariano tried to answer the longings

---

(1) *I Would Be Private*. Rose Macaulay. 1937. Permission to quote secured from Curtis Brown, Ltd.

(2) *Anthony Adverse*. Copyright 1933 by Hervey Allen and reprinted by permission of Rinehart & Company, Inc., Publishers.

of his generation of pleasure-loving Florentines
with no rebuke for their sins, "but entertained
them with classical quotations, philosophy, as-
tronomy, and poetry." He failed—who remembers
his name for any outstanding contribution to
beauty, or as a benefactor of the race? Rather, it
is the task of the preacher to learn from Savonarola who came along with truth and stole the
crowds with an answer they could understand—
which probably went something like this, "Surrender your befuddled minds and pained hearts
to the Physician of Souls, and He will become in
fact *the Light* of the world." Fra Mariano was
fascinated by beauty for beauty's sake. Savonarola
was bent on truth; and beauty and blessing were
added. Savonarola was right. Time has spoken.
We, too, can be right and have time on our side.
We can, if we take first the gift of truth that
Christmas preaches—God's love for this world so
great that He sent His Son—and work out our way
from there, with the inspiration of that truth setting us free to serve beautifully and meaningfully.
We can learn that much from Zechariah at least.
Profound truths about God and man come first.
And in his case it brought on tremors in his soul
that erupted finally in a poetic utterance that
blessed the world with its beauty and significance.
Who knows what God will do for you, what hidden talents will come to light, what blessings you
are meant to convey and will convey when you
learn this first lesson for after-Christmas living?

Truth, however, does not always yield its inspiration and power easily, is not casually mas-

tered. Zechariah, for instance, had a long period of silence enforced on him. "But you," said Gabriel, "you will be silent and unable to speak until this happens." That seems, does it not, to hint at the possibility that one way to truth is through the discipline of silence, the compulsion of listening for a season. In any event, most of us talk too much. Christmas, together with so many other things, is lost because we do not take time to listen in silence. Something important could be learned every hour of the day if we kept our mouths shut and opened our ears wide. There is good sense to be found in the observation that God gave us two ears and one mouth in order to teach us we were to do twice as much hearing as talking. Zechariah had his questions stilled, his activities curtailed, and then, but only after weeks and months had passed, blessed the world with forceful utterances that gave future generations language for its hours of fellowship, with God.

Nor would I boldly and flatly declare that we can all soar to such dizzy heights as did this inspired father of John, but I am saying that silence before God is ofttimes a more productive way to understanding and convictions than idle talk and questions. Silence, indeed, is often the condition for learning. Silence, as a matter of fact, can bring such important truths home into our consciousness as to make our otherwise stupid attempts at beauty—through poetry, music, or the art of goodwill—simply an overflow from the heart of our being, a spontaneous and unstudied gift presented us by truth. Small wonder that Carlyle should write in *Sartor Resartus* (a book which my Professor of Literature urged be read at least once each year) :

Silence is the element in which great things fashion themselves together; that at length they may emerge, full-formed and majestic, into the daylight of life, which they are thenceforth to rule. Not William the Silent only, but all the considerable men I have known, and the most undiplomatic and unstrategic of these, forbore to babble of what they were creating and projecting. Nay, in thy own mean perplexities, do thou thyself but *hold thy tongue for one day:* on the morrow, how much clearer are thy purposes and duties; what wreck and rubbish have those mute workmen within thee swept away, when intrusive noises were shut out! Speech is too often not, as the Frenchman defined it, the art of concealing Thought; but of quite stifling and suspending Thought, so that there is none to conceal.

With Carlyle's near approval, it could be said that even Caliban, deformed slave in *The Tempest,* might have found some good use for speech had he known enough in his savage state to ask big questions and wrestle for answers in silence. But as it was, he rightly complained, "You taught me language; and my profit on't is I know how to curse." Well, raise your questions, but then enforce silence and listen. Do as did Zechariah. That is the second lesson for after-Christmas living. Be sensible enough to walk in the way of the quieted tongue and listening ear if you are bent, as you ought to be, on discovering the meaning for life.

And what did the father of the Baptist learn in silence that found expression in due season in significant forms of beauty that blessed the world? Why, probably the most elementary things, trite things, but important because *he* learned them. They became part of *his* experience, and therefore became the foundation for the assumptions on which he later acted—so he took "a writing-tablet and wrote down, 'His name is John.'" He was overpowered by truth and became its servant.

The first elemental fact that he yielded himself to is expressed in the opening words of his song: "Blessed be the Lord the God of Israel." The clue to its importance is seen in the emphasis which is given this idea in the rest of the song. Notice, for instance how he talks about "the house of his servant David," and "the lips of his prophets," and "his holy covenant." All of this tells us that he had discovered the God of history and the God in history. Oh, to be sure, he had known something about the God of Abraham and Isaac and Jacob long before this dramatic episode. Was he not a priest? Had he not chanted dutifully in the Temple, and faithfully offered the manifold sacrifices in strict conformity to the rites prescribed? All that, of course, and more. He was, furthermore, probably among that incredibly small minority that had gained some limited conception of the spiritual implications of the coming Messiah. It was not enough! As I see it, his trouble was that God for him existed in the far-off places. His God had once been active in the sphere of history but had retired from the conflict, lo, these hundreds of years. God would, to be sure, become active again on behalf of His people, but in the

dim and misty future. For the present, God was
not near, and His ear was all but closed to anxious
and tearful supplication. The best that could be
done, under the circumstances, was to stagger
along with a hope that had become a burden. So
the messenger sent from God, and the message,
became a matter to doubt and to discount, and he
said, "But how am I to be sure of this?" He was
given silence to think things over.

It was not easy to visualize God at work in the
days of Zechariah. Let that be said as a matter of
record. Israel had fallen on evil days. The glory
that belonged to her during the reign of David
was but a vague memory. The God who guided
in smoke and fire was indistinct, a subject that
more and more had the overtone of myth and
legend. And then—this God of the fathers came
alive! It took questions, silent wrestling, sweating
and bleeding in the pit of the brain and heart,
but God was alive. God was there, there in the
dark—Zechariah knew it, knew it in the deep
places where faith dwells, that this God of ancient
history was in Israel's today and would be in her
tomorrow. "Blessed be the Lord the God of Israel,
for He has cared for His people and wrought them
redemption," he sang with an assurance that radiated confidence born of truth.

We, too, have lived and are now living in dark
days. The authority and power of God seem often
but a flimsy idea to toy with and cast aside as
non-essential, non-rational, and non-desirable.
God, if not dead, is most certainly asleep, seems
to be the apathetic conclusion of a listless and

tired world. A key question that can rouse us from
our stupor is: What do you think of history? Has
it meaning? or no? What is your theory? What is
your conviction? Karl Marx gave answer one day
and urged us to believe that economic forces dic-
tate all events; that the end of history is a classless
society. Jean-Paul Sartre, forty-year-old French
philosopher, is captivating great numbers of followers with "a bleak philosophy of pessimism"
called "Existentialism."[3] Scorning the past and
the future (I hope I am being just) he promises
power for living in passive acceptance of mere
and sheer existence. So sorely do we need in our
time a dynamic concept of the meaning of history.

Scripture, we may feel as we read it, hurriedly
examines one personage after another, but upon
closer examination we know that at final last it is
always God who is the chief personage, the chief
actor, and that whether in individual or national
history. God is always before and ahead! His hand
is ever at the controls. The beginning is His, the
now, and the future. Nothing takes place unless
His mysterious power is shaping things. Even
Caesar makes plans that God utilizes to work His
holy will. Now, if we could take hold of that to
steady us, how different the world would become
for us. Zechariah found this truth in finding a
God that cared *now*, and he found Him in personal experience. And it was important—important for him—important enough to guide his life
and decisions and behavior! That can happen to

(3) *Existentialism.* Bernard Frizell. *Life*, June 17, 1946. Quotation by special permission.

us. God hath visited and wrought redemption. We have Christmas with the Incarnation—Immanuel: God with us.

A certain historian, so James Reid tells us, not long ago set himself "to answer the question, Has all this happened before? His answer was that it had. It happened to the people of the Bible, in crisis after crisis of their history. But they had something, he said, which we have lost. They could say 'God is our refuge and strength; therefore we will not fear, though the earth be removed.' If we know," he concludes, "God as the Lord of history, there is no situation that can bring us to despair. We have been there before, and seen God working in it."[4] That confidence is what seized Zechariah, and made his glad optimism possible. A song of victory was possible with gloom and despair around because God's program was marching on, and that program was sound and good and undefeatable. And that optimism can be ours. There is hardly any excuse for our not having this knowledge. We have Christ's Cross to stare at and be won by. Let us not rest until we come to grips with this truth, and know of ourselves that because of the Incarnation

> Christ will be with me all the way,
> Today, tomorrow, every day,
> Till traveling days be ended.

And that will be a third practical lesson for after-

---

(4) *The Indispensable Book*. James Reid, D.D. *The British Weekly*, June 13, 1946. Quotation by special permission.

Christmas living. Nothing, absolutely nothing, can touch you to bring harm and fear if "underneath are the everlasting arms."

The fourth lesson we can learn has to do with God's love. Zechariah sighted God's passionate and holy love, and sang, "He has raised up a strong Savior for us . . . to save us from our foes and from the hand of all who hate us." God makes us important: He comes to save *us!* He is eager to lend His almighty aid in the unequal struggle *we* are engaged in against foes that threaten destruction.

Humanity has been trying to persuade itself that it is animal. We have even bluntly and succinctly put it down in black and white that "man is an animal." Having pounded that home with fiendish glee, we have proceeded to act like animals. It is time, and past time, to call attention to the fact that we are living souls above anything else. We are responsible beings and answerable for what we do and say. Strangely enough, it is not merely God's world, but in a certain sense it is man's world. Within limitations, man controls his destiny. That is the very point that confuses us so often. We sense this truth and are misled by it into a pride that is a false pride and which destroys us. Our true dignity and worth are seen only against the background of God's love. At the Cross is revealed the true manhood of man. We cringe from that revelation because our dull minds fail us when we are asked to behold our true stature as the objects of God's sacrifice. We fling ourselves away from that vision because we can not stand to see the requirements demanded of such a manhood and personality. So we beat a swift retreat into the activities of group and social salvation by organization. It is man being less than man that is troubling this generation. We will not gain a right estimate of personality until we see God at work in and for human beings. It is man alone who casts his vote for destruction or for salvation. Such is the responsibility of the soul to which we must awaken soon if God is to be allowed to make manifest His great salvation in our time.

I count! You count! What you and I do and say, or what you and I do not do and say, is of vital and paramount importance to the world around us and to the God above us. When God wanted to save the world there was this Incarnation, and the appeal of love was directed at *man*. *Man* holds the key to today and tomorrow. He is the key! It is even possible to say with new meaning that it is literally true, and demonstrated to be true by the events of the day, that Christ was right when He said, "Without *me* ye can do nothing," and understand by it that "without *a good man* ye can do nothing." Christ is that good man. Take then the love which He revealed; take then the sacrifice which He made; take then His bold confidence in the world as a moral world in which truth and righteousness prevail because there is a discernment in and with and under this universe that approves what its very nature is, and eschews that which is and stands in wrong relationship with it. The strength and power of good men (Christ's men) is our hope for a humanity that has been given ever new and increasingly heavier responsibilities like atomic power, until now man's jaunty manner is gone, his steps slowed, and his forehead wet with nervous sweat. He knows that his is the responsibility and time is fleeting and destruction awaits—or salvation. And the power of *one* good man counts—you! Remember how in the days of Abraham there came a day when he was pleading with God for the salvation of Sodom? "Then he said, Oh let not the Lord be angry, let me say one word more: suppose ten are to be found in it? I will not sweep it way, he replied, for the sake of the ten." Sodom, that great city, was destroyed because within its confines there could not be found ten good men. A whole city might have been spared if there had been ten good men. Ah! the strength and power of a few good men—what they do and can do for a community or nation—like "leaven," said our Lord in the descriptive way that endeared Him as teacher and friend. Woe! and woe! be to that city or nation that hasn't a few good men to keep it from utter folly. And that strength and that influence is open to you. *"Everyone* who believes in Him may have eternal life, instead of perishing." "Christ liveth in me," said the Apostle as his witness to the fact that this Christ is available! Well, Zechariah counted! His son counted! God dealt with them personally. History means God, the Maker, at work for and with and in persons.

Zechariah discovered that God's active interest in history is salvation. He visualized deceived men enlightened, and freed from slavery to wrong

ideals and false conceits and morbid fears. He
pictured man accepting his responsibility as man,
converted, re-born, and consecrated. He saw man
walking hand in hand with his true destiny as
God's child, a relationship of Father-child made
alive and real in full and complete surrender to
Christ. Hear how beautifully he put it:

> that, freed from fear and from the hand of our foes,
> we should worship him in holiness and uprightness
> all our days within his presence.

These are some of the truths that stirred up the
gift of song in the heart of an old man who worked
out his salvation in silence before God. I warned
you that these truths he learned were elementary
things; important, not because they were new, but
because they were truths that *he* discovered. It
was because *he* experienced them that life became
different for him, and all gloom and fear were
dispelled.

But what he experienced, you can. God does
require that you come seeking truth. "Blessed are
those who hunger and thirst for goodness! They
will be satisfied." God does require that you quit
doing all the talking and learn to listen in and to
silence. But on that road of sincerity and fellowship God still walks in Christ, alive forevermore.
Luther found Him. So did Wesley. And their gifts
of song were released, too, to bless the world and
glorify God. More important is the fact that uncounted thousands have duplicated this very thing
in their lives. We can not call them by name, nor
can we name the songs they sang to enrich the

lives of those about them, but it is safe to say that each brought some gift to God and humanity without which today we should be the poorer. Each in his own way counted, and each did a work for and with God that nobody else could have done. All these found God anxious to save.

And that is the most important lesson of all for after-Christmas living. God is anxious to take *us* and make *us,* and stands, therefore, as our Apostle of Love says He stands, at the door knocking, . . . knocking, . . . knocking.

AMEN

And when eight days were fulfilled for circumcising him, his name was called Jesus, which was so called by the angel before he was conceived in the womb.

LUKE 2:21

Chapter Seventeen

Sanctified Memories and Good Hope

WITH the coming of the New Year comes, on printed page and in word picture, Old Father Time. His hour glass and sickle are at hand and with him the little winged cherub symbolizing the new-born year. These symbolic figures give little help in bidding a glad farewell to the old or a happy welcome to the new year.

Life does speed by. Babies do so quickly become youths, and young people soon become old folks; but to speed from babyhood to senility within a twelve-month is to mock the hurried pace of our pilgrimage and the transiency of our present residence here.

In the Christian sanctuary, however, an exchange of characters takes place each New Year's morning when the Church gathers to worship God in fullness of truth.

Old Father Time still remains. There is no denying the constant falling of the sands in his hour glass nor the calendar leaves from the wall. The record book he carries under his arm is a reality and the sweep of the sickle whose name is death will find attestation in the congregation's record.

But, in the reading of the Gospel for the day, the Past, the Future, and Time itself will be confronted with another child, one who does not grow old and frail and pass from the scene. It is the Babe of Bethlehem named of the angel before His birth with the name Jesus and acclaimed by the believing Church of every generation, "he hath saved his people from their sins."

Thus the festival of the changing years assumes a different character.

With Jesus in the picture we dare to speak of sanctified memories and good hope: memories of the past and hopes for the future. We bring them to the throne of grace that "everlasting consolation and good hope" may make bright the past and illuminate the future.

The Past

In the past is God, changeless, clean, holy, omniscient. Before Him in the open book of remembrance is everything that we have been. In the past is the fullness of time when: "God sent forth his Son made of a woman, made under the law, to redeem them that were under the law" (Gal. 4:4-5).

Eight days from the day He came to bless all the world, comes the day of that ceremony of the Old Testament Covenant which put Him "under the law," the rite of circumcision.

He was thereby not only obligated as an Israel-
ite to keep the Covenant and the Covenant laws,
but obligated by His own divine purpose and by
the name given, to "blotting out the handwriting
of ordinances that was against us, which were contrary to us, and took it out of the way nailing it
to the cross" (Col. 2:14).

Memories, the conscious or subconscious piling
up of the records of life, are the constant output
of daily living. The output cannot be stopped so
long as conscious life continues.

Memory is kind or memory is cruel.

Memory is a sweet companion to the saint in
the latter days of his pilgrimage.

Memory, to him who has sold himself to do
evil, becomes finally like the cadaver chained to
the convict in the old crude days of paganism to
be dragged about as punishment. Lord Byron who
tried it describes:

> What exile from himself can flee?
> To zones though more and more remote;
> Still, still pursues where'er I be
> The blight of life—the demon thought.

Old faces, old scenes, old voices, old tasks, old
blessings can rise up to bless us all over again, or
it can be thus:

> Days, long since sunk in memory, appear
> As scudding clouds upon the winds of March,
>   so drear,
> So foolishness long gone blows 'cross the scene.
> The little good I did, there in the past,
> Is but as scattered rifts in banks of cloud so vast,
> As little patches dimly through the mists are seen.

What has Jesus to do with all this? Some holiday revelers will say, "Nothing! Never mind, time will take care of it all!"

Go then to Father Time and beg him to turn his hour glass that the sands of last year may run through your hands again; you may say, "Please, oh, please, Father Time, turn your glass for me, there is black sand, sand in it which is muddied with evil, there is red sand, sand red with sin, my sin. Please run the hours through again that they may be cleansed!

"Open the book that is under your arm. Turn the pages of the record of the years for me. I wish to erase, to change, to amend the entries!" If Father Time could speak, he could only answer:

> The moving finger writes and having writ,
> Moves on, nor all your piety or wit
> Shall lure it back, to cancel half a line
> Nor all your tears wash out a word of it.

Time can do nothing to sanctify memories.

The Child whose name is Jesus can. Jesus means Savior. Can one go to Him and say: "Please, Master, the sands that have fallen in the hour glass of my life are grimy with selfishness and reddened with hatred, and crimsoned with sin. Turn time backward that memories may be cleansed"? No, He will not turn the flow of time; but He does have jurisdiction in that past which is memory's domain. He will say, "Have you never read the gospel according to Israel: 'Come now and let us reason together, saith the Lord: Though your sins be as scarlet, they shall be as white as snow; though they be red like crimson, they shall be as wool'?" (Isaiah 1:18.)

He does say to the helpless: "Son, be of good cheer, thy sins are forgiven thee." He does stand between the past and the future whenever you draw near the altar of communion, saying, "This is my body, this is my blood, given and shed for you for the remission of your sins."

If the accuser hiding behind the past says: "It is not only in your memory, it is written in the book, the book of God's remembrance! Your record is there, your personal fingerprints are on its smeared pages!" What can Jesus say to that?

He will say, "My son, my daughter, the book of God's remembrance is real. Look at it, look well at it. Now look unto me—see, I draw my wounded hand across its pages. Now look, see the chemistry of God's grace, two reds make white."

Yes, it is as Paul said: God "hath made him to be sin for us, who knew no sin; that we might be made the righteousness of God in him" (II Cor. 5:21).

The Future

What is it? Just more of the same? The same daily grind, repeated details, the same anxieties, cares, weaknesses, trials, aggravations, sinning? No! He who walks with Jesus the Savior across the divide into the future is not just the same. The very process of God's grace which sanctifies memory through the forgiveness of sins works on in Christian progress day by day. Newness of life in Christ means that tomorrow is better than today, today an improvement on yesterday. True it is that evening by evening God's children have need of the Father's mercy seat where many a slip and fall will be confided; but day by day the Christian "puts off the old," like a dirtied coverall left on the garage nail; day by day he will "put on the new man which after God is created in righteous and true holiness."

So each morning and each New Year we may face the future with good hope.

In this aspiration we are not left just to our own resources, to climb as it were by the motive power of our own New Year resolutions. There is in Scripture a good New Year wish which is also a promise, yea, a guarantee: "Now our Lord Jesus Christ himself, and God, even our Father, which hath loved us, and hath given us everlasting consolation and good hope through grace, comfort your hearts, and establish you in every good word and work" (II Thess. 2:16, 17).

Admittedly there is boldness in facing such a world as is ours today and so uncertain an international, inter-racial, economic, social future as confronts us; but in that future God lives and rules and in Him we trust.

But the scythe on the shoulder of Old Father Time, who can escape that? The reaper whose name is death has been very busy. He has had much cooperation. Death-dealing has been the world's principal business for some time now and there are more and bigger possibilities for mass slaughter. Meanwhile the sickle of the reaper continues its normal swing as every issue of every paper will indicate. Though every horizon seems to carry the lurid prophecy of war and destruction, though we stand daily closer to the encroaching margin where the reaper's sickle sweeps by, yet we, the prisoners of hope, turn with confidence to our stronghold.

Child Jesus was circumcised. This bloody Old Covenant rite foretold that Jesus too should come within the sweep of the scythe, not indeed by necessity as paying the wages of sin in which He has a share, not by mere chance nor by the wavering passion of the mob; but by purpose as by consequence that we, His brethren, who stand in bondage through fear of death, might have hope.

Lusin of China must have been surveying the burial mounds of his unhappy country when he wrote this epigram: "I think it is difficult to say whether there is such a thing as hope or not. Hope is like a road in the country; there was never a road, but when many people walk on it, the road comes into existence."

Our good hope for an eternal future is not based on the wishful thinking of a multitude; but on the promises of God's Word on the demonstrated fact of life from the dead on the part of Him, with whom we confront both the past and the future forevermore—even Jesus.

"Verily, verily I say unto you, He that heareth my word, and believeth on him that sent me, hath everlasting life, and shall not come unto condemnation; but is passed from death unto life" (John 5:24).

AMEN

For of his fulness we all received, and grace for grace. For the law was given through Moses; grace and truth came through Jesus Christ. No man hath seen God at any time; the only begotten Son, who is in the bosom of the Father, he hath declared him.

JOHN 1:16-18

Chapter Eighteen

Our Priceless Christ
Is Free

"YOU can't buy a ticket to a North Dakota sunset!" These striking words were spoken by our beloved friend, the late Pastor Carl B. Yl- visaker, to a group of Luther Leaguers. In our commercial age, it is so easy to forget that the most beautiful things of life are free. The pressure of clever advertising by press and radio tends to make us dollar conscious. No bank account is large enough to purchase the exquisite beauty of a star-speckled moonlit sky, the majestic grandeur of the mighty Rockies, the cool sparkling water of the mountain spring or the fresh invigorating air of the northern pines. Thank God that at the beginning of this new year, even in our commer- cial era, the millionaire and the pauper can stand on level ground to exclaim with the psalmist, "O Lord, how manifold are thy works; in wisdom hast thou made them all; the earth is full of thy riches" (Psalm 104:24).

Best of all, life's greatest possession cannot be bought with money. *Our priceless Christ is free.* This is the great truth of our text for this New Year's Day. All the wealth in the world cannot buy the grace of God in Christ which alone can bring life to one immortal soul—rich or poor. This marvelous truth is graphically stated in Isaiah 55:1—"Ho, everyone that thirsteth, come ye to the waters, and he that hath no money; come ye, buy, and eat; yea, come, buy wine and milk without money and without price."

The greatness of Christ, the true Light, the Word made flesh, the only begotten of the Father, is now proclaimed in this great prologue of John's Gospel in our text. To appreciate the gift of our priceless Savior, we must first realize that we are lost in helplessness. This is a hard lesson to learn. Only the Holy Spirit through the Word can bring us to our knees in absolute helplessness. We are helpless, for we have sinned. "The law was given by Moses," states our text. God spoke. Too often this Law of God is too far from our every day experiences. Life becomes different when the ten commandments get into our kitchens, stores, offices, schoolrooms, living rooms, bank accounts, into our Saturday nights. When God becomes real as a living person who sees, hears, knows, understands and at the same time demands nothing less than perfect holiness, then we are gripped by the truth of God that we have not pleased God but have sinned in thought, word, and deed. No matter who he is, when an honest person meets the holy God of the Bible, the one inevitable result

is the prayer, "God be merciful to me a sinner."
This God who demands perfection wants us to
take inventory of this past year. There can be no
flaw in His accounting. He has a record not only
of all our mistakes but of all we have failed to do
for Him. Face your holy God and His demands
on *you* in His holy Law given to Moses in the ten
commandments as you look back over the way
you have lived the year that is closing. If you are
honest with God and honest with yourself, then
you will discover by God's Spirit that you are lost
in helplessness for you have sinned.

In this Law, God wants to wear you out, slay
you and condemn you. Only then will you be
ready to receive and appreciate the *free grace of
God in Christ*. Paul puts it this way in Romans
3:19, 20—"Now we know that what things soever
the law saith—it saith to them who are under the
law, that every mouth may be stopped and all the
world may become guilty before God. Therefore
by the deeds of the law there shall no flesh be justified in his sight for by the law is the knowledge
of sin."

The necessary experience of seeing one's lost,
helpless condition before being able to grasp the
real meaning of grace in Christ was once described graphically by a schoolmaster in Sweden.
He wrote, "I did not realize that grace can not,
nay, will not, save a sinner who still trusts in himself, who is not spiritually naked, who has not
found life in Christ alone but covers himself with
the ragged garments of his own righteousness.
Grace cannot build up the self-righteous. The

idea I had was that the more I labored at my self-improvement, the more certainly I would succeed. Who does not see that this means the soul's refusal of the sacrificial death of our Savior Jesus Christ. 'If righteousness came by the law, then Christ is dead in vain.' The self-righteous Pharisee or, in modern times, the man who trusts for salvation in the development of his 'character,' as he terms the process, is an abomination to the Lord." Many of us have gone through these experiences as we have come to rejoice in the real meaning of God's *free* gift of grace in Christ our Savior for our daily life. The Law was given by Moses that we might be ready to receive the grace and truth that came by Christ. As Paul says, "Wherefore the law was our schoolmaster to bring us unto Christ, that we might be justified by faith" (Gal. 3:24). Let God's unchanging Law grip you, your life, your heart today. Only then will you see that you have sinned, that you are lost in helplessness. Only then will you be ready to receive your priceless Christ who is a free gift from God to you.

Neither can we reach God. It is human to try. The heathen do in their ignorance. The cultured do in their refinement. It is natural for man to try to reach God by pulling himself upward by his own good works, his own efforts. This just cannot be done. God says so. We are helpless. We cannot reach up to Him but, thank God, He came down to us in Christ. This Word, Jesus Christ, says, "I am the Way—no man cometh unto the Father but by me" (John 14:6). May God open our eyes to see that there is a wall that separates us and God

—the wall of our sins. Only then will we rejoice fully in the great truth that only Christ can break down the middle wall and we who sometimes were far off are made nigh by the blood of Christ, for He is our peace (Ephesians 2:13-14) . We are lost in helplessness because we cannot reach God.

Neither can we ever see Him, for in the words of our text—"no man hath seen God at any time." When the helplessness of this truth grips our heart, then and only then are we ready to receive with genuine joy the priceless Christ, God's free gift described in our text as "the only begotten Son, which is in the bosom of the Father, he hath declared him."

Though lost in our own helplessness, we become complete in God's grace as we receive our priceless Christ who is free. Complete in God's grace! What a marvelous contrast to the fact—lost in helplessness. What makes the difference? Only this—our priceless Christ. He alone is the answer to whether your life should be empty or full, dark or light, tragic or joyful, chaotic or orderly. Christ alone can rescue lost, hell-bound sinners for a blessed eternity with God. Receiving grace— the unmerited favor of God—alone can make the difference, "for by grace are ye saved through faith and that not of yourselves, it is the gift of God" (Ephesians 2:8) .

We are complete in His grace, for grace and truth came by Jesus Christ. God did not just tell us about grace and truth. Then He could have used another Moses or prophet. Jesus Himself was grace and truth. Moses may disappear but the law

remains nevertheless. It is given only by Him. But
if you take away Jesus Christ, grace and truth
disappear, for His own person and work consti-
tute the very substance of grace and truth. They
are united in His person. You cannot separate
them. They came through Jesus Christ. Conse-
quently this old world needs more than just to hear
about Jesus Christ or even to know His teachings.
A school man said to me recently, "The youth of
this country need above all to know the teachings
of Christianity." I answered quickly, "Our young
people need more than the teachings of Christianity. They need the person of Jesus Christ, our
crucified and risen Savior who lives today. Without the personal possession of Christ, there can be
no power to live according to the teachings of
Christianity." We can be complete, saved, rescued
in God's grace only as we receive the free gift of
our priceless Savior, for "grace and truth came by
Jesus Christ" according to God's Word in our
text. Do you possess Christ as your Savior today?
That is the most profound question any soul can
ever face.

In Christ we are complete in His grace too, for
it is inexhaustible—His fulness, grace for grace.
God's grace is wide enough and deep enough to
receive the lowest sinner. Jesus is able to save to
the uttermost. He came to seek and to save the
lost. You who stand condemned because you are
not perfect, listen to the sweet message of God's
grace: "There is no condemnation to them who
are in Christ Jesus" (Romans 8:1). You who stand
loaded down with mistakes and failures—look—

"Behold the Lamb of God that taketh away the
sin of the world" (John 1:29). This grace includes you. You who stand ashamed as you behold the stains and blemishes of this past year—
listen to the message of God's grace, "the blood of
Jesus Christ his Son cleanseth us from *all* our
sin" (I John 1:7). You who stand cursed because
you have not continued to do all things written in
the book of the Law, listen—"Christ hath redeemed us from the curse of the law, being made
a curse for us" (Gal. 3:13). This is God's grace
for you and me. Peter had only this same grace on
which to depend as he said in Acts 15:11, "But
we believe that through the grace of the Lord
Jesus Christ we shall be saved, even as they." This
is true of every saint of God who has ever faced
eternity. No one can ever graduate from the
prayer of our beloved hymn,

> Nothing in my hands I bring,
> Simply to Thy Cross I cling,
> Naked, come to Thee for dress,
> Helpless, look to Thee for *grace;*
> Foul, I to the fountain fly,
> Wash me, Savior, or I die.

To grow as a Christian is not to become better
in our own estimation. That would be growth
away from grace and not *in* grace. It is interesting
to observe Paul's analysis of himself. In I Corinthians 15:9 (written about 57 A.D.) he says,
"But I am least of the apostles." In Ephesians 3:8
(about 62-63 A.D.) he says, "Unto me who am
least of all saints." As a climax in I Timothy 1:15
(65 A.D.) he says, "This is a faithful saying, and

worthy of all acceptation, that Christ Jesus came into the world to save sinners; of whom I am chief." The closer we come to God, the more we see our sins and the absolute need of God's grace. Dr. B. M. Christensen of Augsburg College said once to a group of theological students, "Only broken instruments can play in the symphony of God's Kingdom." Only those who pray Psalm 51 from the heart will have the door open for God's grace to enter and to work. Too many people are *trying* to be Christians instead of *trusting* God's powerful grace in Christ. Instead of believing the grace in the heart of God, some seek grace in their own hearts. I know this seems the most logical to the human mind. It is as Dr. Swebelius says, "The law is fairly well known by nature; the gospel, however, is a mystery concealed from reason." Even some who preach fall for the temptation of a "character" religion instead of a religion by grace alone, a religion of trying to live Christ-like lives by one's own effort instead of giving God's grace opportunity to work in the heart. They forget that a sanctified life must have its roots in the daily forgiveness of sin by the grace of God. Otherwise there can not be any power for Christ-likeness. It is the first step—grace alone—yes, the second, too; for all is by grace in Christ. One has said, "grace is the flower, glory is the fruit."

"The Gospel is the Christian's greatest science and highest wisdom, in the study of which he remains a humble student all the days of his life," said Dr. Martin Luther. "But," he continues, "there is this peculiarity about the Gospel, that nothing seems easier to learn. The result is that as soon as a person has heard or read something of it, he imagines that he is master of the subject and is quite ready for something new." Rosenius in his excellent book, *A Faithful Guide to Peace with God,* makes this striking comment, "Such people reason in this way. 'I know very well what I am to believe. I know all about the grace and forgiving love of God in Christ. That has been given once and for all. The matter is clear as daylight. I am satisfied on that subject. But what am I to do? How am I to live? Those are worthwhile questions. Give us the answers to these questions.' " How this description fits many even inside our churches today. Rosenius continues, "Thus they never arrive at the right way of life, the right principle of daily conduct. They have never learned the chief spiritual lack which is life itself, genuine repentance and a living faith in Christ. They do not realize the utter futility of their own works in the matter of justification before God. They have never despaired of themselves nor have they experienced the meaning and power of true faith. For in that case they would not say that they have had enough of the Gospel. They would rather say, as God's Word and experience verify, that only in the knowledge of God and His unbounded grace lie the power and joy of leading a truly God-pleasing life." The sweetest message that the Christian wants to hear daily is the gospel—the good news that Christ died and rose again that man may have forgiveness of sins by His blood and live in that daily cleansing as a child of God. Only when a sinner has received forgiveness of sins for nothing, for absolutely nothing, is he ready to give all honor, glory and praise to the crucified Savior who was slain for our sins. Then the grace of God is real for salvation and for daily living. Only then can God's grace use us effectively to witness and to work for Him. This was the apostle Paul's experience who said, "But by the grace of God I am what I am: and his grace which was bestowed upon me was not in vain; but I labored more abundantly than they all: yet not I, but the grace of God which was with me" (I Corinthians 15:10).

Grace for grace—what a marvelous picture. Inexhaustible as the mountain spring! As wave follows upon wave on the mighty ocean, so grace ever new and ever greater follows grace, one measure assures another. "But he giveth more grace" (James 4:6). We have not purchased or deserved it but God confers it freely as a free gift. What can be a more glorious message for the Christian as he steps out into an unknown year, with its trials, dangers, uncertainties? Grace for grace! "But where sin abounded, grace did much more abound" (Romans 6:20). "And he said, My grace is sufficient for thee" (II Corinthians 12:9). Complete in His inexhaustible abundant grace according to our text—"and of his fulness have all we received and grace for grace." This comes alone as a free gift to every repentant sinner through our priceless Christ. Paul said of Him, "For ye know the grace of our Lord Jesus Christ,

that though he was rich, yet for your sakes he
became poor, that ye through his poverty might
be rich" (II Corinthians 8:9).

In Christ we are complete in His grace too, for
we have seen God. What a glorious New Year's
message! In the words of our text, "the only begotten Son, which is in the bosom of the Father,
he hath declared him." If you want to know
God, get next to Jesus Christ. He is God. How our
scientific age needs this truth today! In His own
words, He says, "He that hath seen me hath seen
the Father" (John 14:9). What more do you
want?

Christ must become our possession and prop-
erty if we are to partake of His grace and become
a power in this wicked world. Many of you received Him in holy Baptism. Is He yours today?
Without Christ, you are lost. Are you depending
only on Christ, your Savior, God's free gift to you,
for your salvation, you who deserve only punishment and shame because you are lost in helplessness? In yourself you cannot please God, you cannot reach God, you cannot see God. I would be
afraid to start a new year if I did not know from
God's own unchanging promise that I am complete in God's grace. This privilege is yours. The
door of grace is open yet. Some day it will be
closed. Today, now, Jesus Christ says to you,
"Come unto me, all ye that labor and are heavy
laden and I will give you rest" (Matthew 11:28).
He also adds, "Him that cometh unto me I will
in no wise cast out" (John 6:37). Claim Christ
now so you will be complete in His grace today,

for grace and truth came by Jesus Christ and His grace is inexhaustible. Complete in His grace you will see God now by faith and soon face to face. Today is the day of grace. Tomorrow may be too late. In the words of Luther, "Let us live as though Christ were crucified yesterday, risen today, and coming tomorrow."

Our priceless Christ is free! Salvation and life can not be bought. God's grace is for you today. May our response be in the words of our beautiful hymn:

> By *grace* alone shall I inherit
> That blissful home beyond the skies.
> Works count for naught, the Lord incarnate
> Hath won for me the heav'nly prize,
> Salvation by His death He wrought,
> His *grace* alone my pardon bought."

In Jesus' Name, AMEN

He spake also this parable: A certain man had a fig tree planted in his vineyard; and he came seeking fruit thereon, and found none. Then said he unto the vinedresser, Behold, these three years I come seeking fruit on this fig tree, and find none: cut it down; doth it also cumber the ground? And he answering saith unto him, Lord, let it alone this year also, till I shall dig about it, and dung it: and if it bear fruit thenceforth, well; but if not, thou shalt cut it down.

LUKE 13:6-9

Chapter Nineteen

This Year Also

THE world is a spiritual jungle. Fierce question marks stalk the peace of man. We crave deliverance from its snarling uncertainties. We are not satisfied with its daily newspaper for a Bible. We want none of its screaming headlines for our New Year's gospel. In the year which lies before us we shall need more than new ways of fretting and new places in which to toss.

We need to entrust our futures into the Pierced Hands. We need to rest our weight on living Truth. We need the leverage of a solid rock. We need to set our feet upon God's settled fact. Only thus can we fare forth unafraid.

The year before us is a *"year of our Lord."* In this let us find our confidence. It will be a great year to the degree that great truths find willing men. Let us sense that our days are the planted possibilities of God. Let us pray for awareness, that we may not miss the unobtrusive miracles of each passing hour. Let us remember that *to love life apart from God is to be in love with death!*

We crave assurance this New Year's Day. We can be sure before our open Bible, for in it we have a substantial basis for a shock-proof faith and an all-weather joy. In it we find truths which have borne the weight of many lives, facts which are unhaunted by any question mark. Here is one: "For God so loved the world, that he gave his only begotten Son, that whosoever believeth in him should not perish, but have everlasting life" (John 3:16). And another: "If we confess our sins, he is faithful and just to forgive us our sins, and to cleanse us from all unrighteousness" (I John 1:9). And still another: "The Lord is my shepherd; I shall not want" (Psalm 23).

Christ has many earthly amplifiers for His heavenly truths, sometimes a cradle and sometimes a casket, one day a joy and another a sorrow, but today just the quiet tick of a clock and the crisp clean surface of a new calendar. The clock and the calendar—what effective preachers they are! How they level the proud and humble the haughty! How they chide the sluggard and shame the cheat! How well they serve to give point and power to this parable of our Lord!

There is something sobering about the quiet tick of a faithful clock, something searching about the very whiteness of a new calendar. The flight of time has a sobering effect on every thoughtful man.

In this morning's text Christ throws wide one of heaven's windows and bids us tarry outside to overhear Love's conversation, a conversation born of concern not for fig trees but for men, for this is essentially a *repentance parable*. There is history in it, the history of a chosen nation, of God's careful cultivation, of a high-priestly intercession, and a sad rejection—the history of Israel and the earthly ministry of our Lord.

But there is more than history. There is warning and there is prophecy. Through this parable the clock and the calendar speak with emphasis of Love's holy purpose, of Love's gracious providence, of Love's rightful expectation, of Love's careful inspection, of Love's sad disappointment, of Love's withheld condemnation, of Love's patient cultivation, and of Love's final separation. In summary they tell us that:

1. Love is purposeful to produce.
2. Love is patient to cultivate.
3. Love is powerful to separate.

In one word Christ's challenge to each one of us today is: "Repent!" The opening of a year is always a repentance reminder, for repentance alone can turn foliage into fruit. Prayerless, indeed, is the man who can take down an old calendar without an upward look. The new year is God's silent rebuke to the fruitless and His searching encouragement to the fruitful. To the former it says: "About face . . . Bear fruit!" To the latter: "Press on . . . Bear more!"

When God would usher in His Kingdom He chose a great man and gave to him a very great word. We read of it in the third chapter of the Gospel according to Luke. The man was John the Baptist and the word was "repent." So well did John speak it that very soon his listeners were asking: "What shall we *do?*" To the people John replied: "Keep only one coat. . . . Share your dinner!" To the publicans he said: "Mend your business ways. . . . Don't over-reach for profits!" To the soldiers: "Don't be brutes. . . . Be content with your wages!" Such homely advice! Such disconcertingly simple replies! Such embarrassingly practical things to do! Things that couldn't be put off or admired from a distance, things that couldn't be lost in discussion but demanded action, things that found them where they lived and urged them to start from where they were! Such is always the case when repentance is liberated from the dictionary and permitted to walk the streets of life. Truly, repentance is as practical as life itself.

Historically, this parable is God's New Year's sermon written large upon the spacious walls of time. It tells us that God measures time in Kingdom progress, that history is but the sure movement of a very patient but altogether purposeful Father. It reminds us that God measures worth in fulfilled purpose, that He is never aimless and never for a moment helpless, that He is on the march in the lives of nations and of men.

The place of privilege is a place of probation. It is always tenanted, never controlled. The hour for fruit-bearing is a fleeting hour. God plants His holy possibilities, then waters them with His mercy. He is unsatisfied with foliage, for He has provided for fruit. Each inspection is followed by a patient cultivation. Searching events are for self-examination. Great crises are not blind catastrophes. They are rather kind approaches from above. God's hand of love is held out still, but where men grow increasingly brittle, the nation finally breaks in the hand that would bless it. It is the end of another era. Another tower of Babel crumbles into dust. Another proud nation is laid away.

Yes, historically, this parable tells us that our proud young nation, this leafy branch which is America, is on trial. It faces us with the fact that the only way from foliage to fruit is via Calvary, and the hour is very late!

Personally, I must know this, that God's mercy is my only opportunity. In a world of sin it may be said that mercy is the very stuff of which time is made. The key to God's future is a blood-rusted key. It is the key called *pardon*. But the path to pardon is always repentance, the turning from sin to the Savior, the godly sorrow which leads to heavenly joy.

The prelude to everything great is *repentance*. There never was a spiritual life which did not begin in it. There never can be a successful day which does not include the death of the old and the birth of the new. Truly, the old man must "daily be drowned and die." Only he who is crucified and risen in Christ can bear fruits "worthy of repentance," and only such fruits are pleasing to God. Death to the old means life to the new. The New Year isn't really new unless the man is. Merely changing the calendar never put fruit on life's vines. Christians are not old men who have turned over a new leaf, but new men who have been gripped by Life.

Love Is Purposeful to Produce

This is God's world. God is in it. He wasn't let in. He broke in. He wasn't chosen. He chose it in Christ. He who is above, within, and beyond each passing moment is in this world through His Son. Other things will come in 1947 models and revised editions, but not God, for God is love and love will never be amended, suspended, or repealed.

Since God is love His purpose is also love. That purpose is the expression of itself to and through its beloved. In one word, fellowship. Days are invitations to the great adventure of growing in love for God and the things of God. But no man can do this until he has seen sin from God's side and lifted a sinner's heart to the God of grace. To grow in grace is to walk in the daily forgiveness of sins. Truly, then, God's mercy is my only opportunity. Verily, there is mercy in each sunrise. There is patience in every dawn. There is divine invitation in the tick of the clock. Therefore we must begin and continue at the altar this New Year. We have a God of new beginnings, a Lord of patient love. How else can we account for our new calendars today?

There is a question oft asked on earth which will never be asked in heaven: "What time is it?" But the silent march of time is clearly discernible through each sentence of this parable. *"These three years . . . this year also . . . then, after that"—*

all of these phrases serve to make us clock-conscious as we hear the words of our Lord. One finds in them the urgency of our working God. But the tick of the clock is life's most tantalizing distraction to the man who is bent on serving self. In it he finds a reminder of the very limited character of his reign, the final verdict on the utter insignificance of his most elaborate personal plan.

The Christian, too, is sometimes distressed by the silent invincibility of time, partly because he has not yet been fully educated into the heart and mind of Christ, but partly because of his new-born love for the will and work of God and his new passion for God's Kingdom both in heaven and on earth. He sees so much to do, so little done.

But to the Christian the tick of the clock has its beauty, too. Underneath the unmusical sameness of its mechanical sound he hears the hidden harmonies of that shoreless land and that spacious home, the place where none need measure time for all are free from its ravages and where they never speak of past and future for they are gripped in the joy of an endless present. Yes, to the Christian the clock and the calendar speak the language of hope fulfilled, of faith which has become sight, and of God's prophecy come true.

How often we speak of tomorrow! Yet tomorrow is the most presumptuous of subjects, except in the Name of Him who holds all of the tomorrows in the hollow of His pierced hand. Tomorrow is the enemy of the man who refuses to make friends with God. It suggests the slow consumption of all that he is feverishly set to defend, the subtle disintegration of all that the natural man holds dear. Truly, "tomorrow" is the most ominous word in the dictionary of the uncommitted man.

As a sinner I will bring to God my confession this New Year's Day. As one who is forgiven I will ask for continued grace to grow in obedience and love. Daily will He help me to make His eternal arrangement my personal choice. Then can I be certain that this new year is a gift with the well-wishes of the Giver. I need not know all of the details since I know my destination. I will plant my feet on the solid rock of God's nature; I will rest my head on the soft pillow of His providence; I will live my life under the undimmed radiance of His promise.

Love Is Patient to Cultivate

Every flippant sinner is a walking demonstration of the patience of God. Every gay and gaudy vice is but a testimony to the tempered strength of this world's Ruler. Dry-eyed transgression is never a proof of God's favor. Nor is it evidence of any weakness on our Lord's behalf. *This year, also* . . . God has said it again. Will He say it next year? No one knows. Again this day our High Priest prays. Another year is ours in which to repent.

God still does marvelous things. He still makes His home in every heart where He is given working-room. He still honors His Word. He still answers prayer. He still stands on His promises. He still forgives all who will be forgiven. So gracious is He that He not only invades our death with His perfect life, but gives us a place at His work-bench, too. He offers to build His Kingdom with ex-convict labor. He gives us something to do!

But time does not only pass. It *confirms!* The traffic of the hours and days wears little ruts into graves and little upward trails of well-done duty into highways to the throne of God. He who has called us into fellowship has also entrusted to us a *stewardship*. Casual Christianity is the prickliest thorn in His crown. That half-covered yawn on the face of man in the face of God . . . this is the grief of heaven and the curse of earth. An unfruit-ful presence is an expense to God's Kingdom. It is a sin for a man who won't serve to take up space in this tired world. He makes of the world a crowded place. The years are God's patient culti-vations of us all. He has provided for fruit. He expects fruit. He inspects for fruits today.

Love Is Powerful to Separate

It is in the nature of love to protect its beloved. Therefore our God who is love must judge the unrepentant. Heaven could no longer be heaven with one single sin let in. The purpose of judg-ment is separation and the purpose of separation is protection. He who purposes to build a king-dom must exclude as well as include. There is judgment in New Year's Day.

There was a today which knew no yesterday. There will be a today which shall know no tomor-row. *Jesus is coming again.* Time carries us closer to that day which shall reveal the total bankruptcy of this world's best, the day which shall be the full and final vindication of the will and works of God. To the Christian time is God's Home-bound chariot carrying him closer to his shining goal.

The clock strikes twelve in the life of every man. The final crisis arrives and the man is seen for what he really is. The chain of choices becomes a chain of consequences. Like all crises, this one does not so much make the man as measure him.

This parable speaks especially to us who are spiritually privileged. It reminds us that the sun sets on the day of grace. Privileges cannot be abused forever. In a world where God is counting on us inactivity is not neutrality. It is *spiritual mutiny*. Uselessness is the devil's service. Finally, this parable tells us that spurned opportunities become condemning impossibilities. Neglect of talent leads to loss of capacity. "Won't" becomes "Can't," and open doors become iron bars. *There is a wideness in God's mercy but there is also that other side of love which is righteous wrath.*

"But the fruit of the Spirit is love, joy, peace, longsuffering, gentleness, goodness, faith, meekness, temperance: against such there is no law."

AMEN